ETHICAL PRINCIPLES IN THE CONDUCT OF RESEARCH WITH HUMAN PARTICIPANTS

Ad hoc Committee on Ethical Standards
in Psychological Research

Published by

American Psychological Association, Inc.
1200 Seventeenth Street, N. W.
Washington, D. C. 20036

These principles were adopted by the Council of Representatives of the American Psychological Association, December 1972.

73-176058

TABLE OF CONTENTS

5 2 5

The Ethical Principles 1

I. Method Followed in Development of the Ethical Principles 1

II. Introduction and Summary Statement 7

The Scientific Obligation 7

Ethical Dilemmas in Research with Human Participants 8

Elements of the Ethical Conflict 10

Two General Considerations Regarding Research with Human Beings 10

Balancing Considerations For and Against Research That Raises
Ethical Issues 11

Correcting the Investigator's Bias 12

Individual Responsibility and Collegial Review 13

Responsibility for Assistants 14

Differing Research Contexts That Affect the Judgment of Relative
Gains and Costs 14

Ethical Issues Related to the Social Context of Psychological Research 15

III. Commentary on the Ethical Principles 18

Section 1-2. The Decision For or Against Conducting a Given
Research Investigation 18

Incidents 20

Principles 21

Discussion 22

Section 3-4. Obtaining Informed Consent to Participate (Including
Issues of Concealment and Deception) 27

Incidents 28

Principles 29

Discussion 29

Section 5. Assuring Freedom from Coercion to Participate   39

    Incidents   41

    Principle   41

    Discussion   42

Section 6. Fairness and Freedom from Exploitation in the Research

    Relationship   52

    Incidents   53

    Principle   53

    Discussion   54

Section 7. Protection from Physical and Mental Stress   58

    Incidents   59

    Principle   61

    Discussion   61

Section 8-9. Responsibilities to Research Participants following

    Completion of the Research   75

    Section 8   75

        Incidents   76

        Principle   76

        Discussion   77

    Section 9   81

        Incidents   82

        Principle   83

        Discussion   83

Section 10. Anonymity of the Individual and the Confidentiality

    of Data   87

    Incidents   88

    Principle   89

    Discussion   89

IV. Ethical Issues in the Sponsorship of Research, in the Misuse of

    Research, in Restricting Access to Research Findings, and in

    the Utilization of Research Results   98

Ethical Issues Arising in Connection with the Source of Financial
     Support   98
Ethical Issues Raised by the Possibility the Research Might Promote
     Undesirable Forces in Society   100
Ethical Problems in Restricting Access to Research Data   103
Responsibility for Promoting the Utilization of Research Results . .   104

THE ETHICAL PRINCIPLES

The decision to undertake research should rest upon a considered judgment by the individual psychologist about how best to contribute to psychological science and to human welfare. The responsible psychologist weighs alternative directions in which personal energies and resources might be invested. Having made the decision to conduct research, psychologists must carry out their investigations with respect for the people who participate and with concern for their dignity and welfare. The Principles that follow make explicit the investigator's ethical responsibilities toward participants over the course of research, from the initial decision to pursue a study to the steps necessary to protect the confidentiality of research data. These Principles should be interpreted in terms of the context provided in the complete document offered as a supplement to these Principles.

1.   In planning a study the investigator has the personal responsibility to make a careful evaluation of its ethical acceptability, taking into account these Principles for research with human beings. To the extent that this appraisal, weighing scientific and humane values, suggests a deviation from any Principle, the investigator incurs an increasingly serious obligation to seek ethical advice and to observe more stringent safeguards to protect the rights of the human research participant.

2.   Responsibility for the establishment and maintenance of acceptable ethical practice in research always remains with the individual investigator. The investigator is also responsible for the ethical treatment of research participants by collaborators, assistants, students, and employees, all of whom, however, incur parallel obligations.

3.   Ethical practice requires the investigator to inform the participant of all features of the research that reasonably might be expected to influence willingness to participate and to explain all other aspects of the research about which the participant inquires. Failure to make full disclosure gives added emphasis to the investigator's responsibility to protect the welfare and dignity of the research participant.

4.   Openness and honesty are essential characteristics of the relationship between investigator and research participant. When the methodological requirements of a study necessitate concealment or deception, the investigator is required to ensure the participant's understanding of the reasons for this action and to restore the quality of the relationship with the investigator.

1

5.   Ethical research practice requires the investigator to respect the individual's freedom to decline to participate in research or to discontinue participation at any time.   The obligation to protect this freedom requires special vigilance when the investigator is in a position of power over the participant.   The decision to limit this freedom increases the investigator's responsibility to protect the participant's dignity and welfare.

6.   Ethically acceptable research begins with the establishment of a clear and fair agreement between the investigator and the research participant that clarifies the responsibilities of each.   The investigator has the obligation to honor all promises and commitments included in that agreement.

7.   The ethical investigator protects participants from physical and mental discomfort, harm, and danger.   If the risk of such consequences exists, the investigator is required to inform the participant of that fact, secure consent before proceeding, and take all possible measures to minimize distress.   A research procedure may not be used if it is likely to cause serious and lasting harm to participants.

8.   After the data are collected, ethical practice requires the investigator to provide the participant with a full clarification of the nature of the study and to remove any misconceptions that may have arisen.   Where scientific or humane values justify delaying or withholding information, the investigator acquires a special responsibility to assure that there are no damaging consequences for the participant.

9.   Where research procedures may result in undesirable consequences for the participant, the investigator has the responsibility to detect and remove or correct these consequences, including, where relevant, long-term aftereffects.

10.   Information obtained about the research participants during the course of an investigation is confidential.   When the possibility exists that others may obtain access to such information, ethical research practice requires that this possibility, together with the plans for protecting confidentiality, be explained to the participants as a part of the procedure for obtaining informed consent.

I. METHOD FOLLOWED IN DEVELOPMENT
OF THE ETHICAL PRINCIPLES

Since the initial formulation and adoption of the APA code of ethics in 1953, much has changed in the science and the profession, and in the broader social context in which psychologists carry out their activities. New issues have come to the fore, and old issues have reappeared in new guises. A major cluster of ethical issues, where complex new considerations face psychologists, concerns the conduct of research with human research participants.

New research fields have emerged that raise special problems about the relationship of investigator to research participant and about desirable and acceptable procedures. The growing scale of psychological research with human beings has also, of course, brought these issues under increased public discussion and review. New regulations of the U. S. Department of Health, Education, and Welfare state that "No grant involving human subjects at risk will be made to an individual unless he is affiliated with or sponsored by an institution which can and does assume responsibility for the protection of the subjects involved." Such regulations are only one indication of the public interest in how scientists resolve these issues. Congressional hearings on invasion of privacy are another. Hence, both our own needs as psychologists for workable research guidelines and pressures arising from public concern call for reconsideration of ethics in research with human participants in the light of contemporary practice and current dilemmas.

To initiate this reconsideration, the APA Board of Directors appointed an Ad hoc Committee on Ethical Standards in Psychological Research. The method used by the Committee in its work was patterned after that developed by the first APA ethics committee, chaired by Nicholas Hobbs. This method has two distinctive characteristics: The first is that the members of the profession supply ethical problems as raw materials for the formulation of ethical principles. The second is that proposed principles are discussed widely throughout the profession prior to their revision and final adoption. By following this method, the APA became the first—and to our knowledge remains the only—society to have developed a code of ethics by means of empirical and participatory principles.

The ethical principles which were the product of the Hobbs Committee's work have served the Association well; we followed in its methodological footsteps with confidence. We were convinced that doing so would have two major advantages: First, by beginning with ethical problems supplied by the members, we could be confident that the principles at which we finally arrived would be relevant to the everyday issues of contemporary research. Second, the participation of the membership in identifying ethical issues, and subsequently in discussing and revising the proposed principles, should aid us all in becoming more sensitive to ethical issues and in moving toward consensus on good research practice.

In preparing the first published draft of the proposed principles (*APA Monitor,* 1971, **2**(7), 9-28), the Committee carried out a number of operations. These are described briefly in the following paragraphs.

Following a review of the available literature on research ethics, several steps were taken to collect from APA members descriptions of research involving ethical issues in the investigator's conduct toward the research participants. A pilot survey was carried out on a sample of 1,000 members; its primary purpose was to pretest the questionnaires to be used in the larger survey. After revising the questionnaires, research descriptions were solicited from a sample of one-third of the membership, that is, about 9,000 members. From this group we received approximately 2,000 descriptions of research involving ethical questions concerning the treatment of participants.

The question asked of this material was "What are the ethical problems which run through the different studies?" We sought the answer by grouping the studies in categories which shared a common ethical issue. Each issue identified in this way became a target for an attempt to draft an appropriate ethical principle.

The first effort to draft a set of principles revealed gaps and inadequacies in our supply of research descriptions. Our knowledge of the ethics literature as well as our own experience told us that we were short of descriptions, for example, of research in community psychology, of survey research, of research with children, of research on sensitivity training groups, etc. To remedy this we solicited additional research descriptions. This time, in addition to a second sample of 9,000 from the APA membership, we sent special requests to selected groups, for example, to the entire membership of the Division of Developmental Psychology.

This second survey brought approximately 3,000 additional research descriptions. These were combined with the initial 2,000. Together they made what seemed to be an adequate base of raw material from which to proceed.

The Committee also made use of a second major source of information about ethical problems, namely, the experience of scientists with a high level of exposure to a variety of research projects and a history of concern with ethical issues. We identified five groups of persons answering this description: (*a*) journal editors, (*b*) staff members of research review panels, (*c*) directors of large research organizations, (*d*) writers on research ethics, and (*e*) leaders in specialized research areas such as hypnosis. Committee members interviewed 35 such informants.

The remaining task was to draft—and redraft—the ethical principles. Because we were working with material wherein conflicts in values were the rule rather than the exception, this was a lengthy process. In the summer of 1970, for example, Committee members spent a full month in the drafting process.

As noted above, distribution of the first draft of the proposed principles initiated a process of review and criticism by APA members. Discussions were scheduled at many of the 1971 meetings of the regional psychological associations and at the 1971 APA Convention. State and city associations were asked to arrange for local discussions. APA divisions assigned committees to review the principles. The Society for Experimental Social Psychology discussed them at length at its 1971 annual meeting. Psychology departments in colleges, universities, medical schools, research institutes, hospitals, clinics, government agencies, etc.—800 in all—received letters requesting a group discussion of the proposed principles. From each such session the Committee asked that recorders relay suggestions for revision.

In addition, individual psychologists actively interested in research ethics, for example, those who have published on this topic, were asked for their suggestions. By this step, the Committee made sure that it would be exposed to the criticism of those with widely differing viewpoints. Also, through the *Monitor,* an appeal went to all members to tell us what problems we had failed to cover, how the principles fell short of useful guidance and how they might be changed.

These requests for assistance from psychologists were paralleled by consultations with persons in other disciplines. In some cases this took place through written reviews, in others, through face-to-face meetings with the Committee. Included in these consultations were anthropologists, economists, lawyers, philosophers, psychiatrists, and sociologists.

The response was extensive and constructive. Approximately 200 groups scheduled discussions and requested reprints to use for this purpose. A record of reactions and suggestions was received from 120 of these groups. These reactions were supplemented by helpful letters from approximately 75 individual psychologists. The National Council of Chairmen of Graduate Departments of Psychology appointed a committee on research ethics (Rudolph W. Schulz, Chairman; Martin Katahn; Gregory Kimble; Robert Sommer; Rains Wallace), and this group spent a day discussing the proposed principles with the drafting committee.

Working with the reactions from all these sources, the Committee prepared a new draft of proposed principles. This was published in the May 1972 issue of the *APA Monitor* 1972, **3**(5), I-XIX.

Again the Committee actively sought the reactions of APA members. Letters soliciting suggestions went to approximately 800 psychological groups and to all individuals who had made suggestions regarding the July 1971 draft. The *APA Monitor* carried a request for comments to all its readers.

Unlike the response to the 1971 draft, that to the 1972 draft was very light. Two things characterized the comments received. First, many correspondents, both individual and group, who had had reservations about the 1971 draft reported themselves as quite satisfied with the 1972 draft. Their suggestions for change, when made, were within the framework of the new draft.

Second, some of our colleagues who had felt that the 1971 version of the proposed principles failed to prohibit, unqualifiedly, research activities they believed to be harmful to research participants continued to express objections to parts of the 1972 version. To some of them the new draft seemed to have moved even further in the direction of permitting research behavior they considered to be unethical. Some, on the other hand, indicated their appreciation of the difficulty of accommodating divergent emphases within the profession and were reconciled to the 1972 proposals as the best that could win general acceptance at this point in history.

In view of the general level of acceptance of the May 1972 draft of proposed principles, it seemed inappropriate to subject the proposals to yet another major revision. Accordingly, this version of our report is quite similar to the May 1972 revision.

We recommend for adoption by the Association the 10 principles and the accompanying preamble, with the understanding that, as a new component of Ethical Standards of Psychologists, it will undergo mandatory review at five-year intervals.

We recommend, in addition, that the full report be published in order to place the Principles in a context that we believe would be suitable for educational purposes. We recommend further that the report, when published, be distributed to the members of the Association.

Ad hoc Committee on Ethical Standards
in Psychological Research
    Stuart W. Cook, Chairman
    Leslie H. Hicks
    Gregory A. Kimble
    William T. McGuire
    Phil H. Schoggen
    M. Brewster Smith

II. INTRODUCTION AND SUMMARY STATEMENT

The ethical problems of psychological research on human beings are intrinsic to the research enterprise. They follow from the very nature of scientific inquiry when it is applied to human research participants rather than from evil intent or from callousness to human values on the part of the researcher. Almost any psychological research with humans entails some choice as to the relative weights to be given to ethical ideals, some choice of one particular ethical consideration over others. For this reason, there are those who would call a halt to the whole endeavor, or who would erect barriers that would exclude research on many central psychological questions. But for psychologists, the decision not to do research is in itself a matter of ethical concern since it is one of their obligations to use their research skills to extend knowledge for the sake of ultimate human betterment.

Granted that the ethical conflicts that arise in human psychological research are intrinsic, they nevertheless can and should be faced directly and responsibly. Psychologists are rightly held to account for the ethical adequacy of their decisions in the light of the competing values and ethical considerations that are involved. Ultimately, we should be concerned with and judge the ethical quality of the overall decision, rather than passing final judgment on its particular components in isolation.

The purpose of this examination of ethical considerations and principles that arise in the actual course of planning and conducting psychological research with human beings is to promote explicit attention to these ethical issues in their full complexity, and thus to foster responsible decisions.

The Scientific Obligation

We begin with the commitment that the distinctive contribution of scientists to human welfare is the development of knowledge and its intelligent application to appropriate problems. Their underlying ethical imperative, thus, is to carry forward their research as well as they know how.

Since it is rarely possible to predict the uses to which scientific knowledge can be put, the scientist should not be asked to limit research to topics that appear to have immediate relevance to human and social problems. Nor should every research scientist be held responsible for making research applications. In the social division of labor, some scientists can appropriately specialize in the advancement of knowledge. Needless to say, it is often true that research having immediate applications contributes as well to scientific progress.

The importance of psychological research in the overall effort to solve individual and societal problems is a matter of opinion. Most psychologists feel it to be an important component of this effort; few would argue that research alone would suffice. But since research is the scientist's distinctive way to contribute to human welfare, he has an obligation to pursue it to the best of his ability. Implied in this obligation is the psychologist's responsibility to choose wisely where to invest his research efforts, taking into account the potential theoretical significance of the knowledge sought and all relevant information about what it might contribute to human welfare.

Ethical Dilemmas in Research with Human Participants

The specialized perspective of the scientist inevitably creates ethical dilemmas, if only because scientific knowledge and techniques that can be used for human betterment can usually be turned to manipulative and exploitative purposes as well. Just as the results of research in atomic physics can be used both for destructive weapons and for the treatment of cancer, so methods discovered to reduce prejudice toward minority groups, to eliminate trouble-some behavior problems, or to facilitate learning in school may also be used to manipulate political allegiance, to create artificial wants, or to reconcile the victims of social injustice to their fate. The double-edged potentiality of scientific knowledge poses ethical problems for all scientists, psychologists included. To the extent that psychological research deals with important problems and potent methods, psychologists must recognize and alert others to the fact that its potential for misuse grows with its potential for constructive application.

But the psychologist whose research involves human participants faces a special set of dilemmas. The obligation to advance the understanding of significant aspects of human experience and behavior is especially likely to impinge upon well-recognized human rights. Significant research is likely to deal with variables and methods that touch upon sensitive human concerns. And if ambiguity in causal inference is to be reduced to a minimum—an essential of good science—research must be designed in ways that, on occasion, may make the relationship between the psychologist and the human research participant fall short of commonly held ideals for human relationships. Observation of human beings may sometimes violate privacy. Experimentation involving them may have effects upon them to which they have not knowingly agreed.

We consider here several distinguishable respects in which the attempt to do good research on important problems may create ethical dilemmas for the psychologist:

In the first place, psychological research often demands the observation and manipulation of powerful and significant independent variables that make a difference in the world outside the laboratory. Answers to important psychological questions may require that people be subjected to pain, or failure, or other forms of stress, or that they be given drugs that could have harmful effects, or that they undergo influence procedures that could result in enduring change or at least violate their autonomy in the short run.

On the dependent variable side, research often involves the study of profound behavioral effects, since the humanly important independent variables are ones that produce humanly important effects. So fear, embarrassment, aggression, blind conformity, cheating, and boredom as well as the positive aspects of human experience and performance become objects of study. The same considerations require the study of partially dependent groups—children, the psychologically disturbed and incompetent, the poor, the old, and the handicapped. Some of the most serious ethical questions arise from the study of important problems in human contexts such as these.

Not only do ethical questions follow from the psychologist's pursuit of important independent and dependent variables but the methods that are adequate to make inferences as unambiguous as possible tend to be the ones that raise ethical difficulties. Many psychologists believe (although some question this) that to obtain valid and generalizable data, it is often essential that the research participants be naive. The requirements of research may thus seem to demand that the participants be unaware of the fact that they are being studied, or unaware of what is being studied or of the hypotheses under investigation. Or deception may appear to be necessary if a psychological reality is to be created under experimental conditions that permit valid inference.

Progress in science often seems to require the study of component processes in limited and artificial situations. So experimental tasks or environments may sometimes be meaningless, boring, or otherwise unattractive to the research participant. Also, data must sometimes be recorded and preserved for scientific purposes that could later be used to the participant's disadvantage or at least for purposes to which they might object. Or the need to obtain observations on a random sample for the sake of statistical generalization may be in conflict with the ideal of voluntary and informed participation in the research. Controlled comparisons may require withholding treatment from some participants that might possibly be beneficial to them. This inventory of problems could be greatly extended, and is so extended in the discussion of principles to follow.

Practices such as those just mentioned (failure to obtain informed consent, deception, exposure to stress and possible harm, invasion of privacy, withholding of potentially beneficial experiences from members of a control group) raise important ethical issues. Responsible psychologists will obviously avoid using them in pointless and unnecessary ways. They will invest their ingenuity in discovering ways of conducting research that avoid or minimize these problems. But the ethical dilemma with which the research psychologist is confronted includes not only the negative side—ways in which the dictates of good research come in conflict with particular ethical ideals. It also includes obligations to advance knowledge of human consciousness and behavior. If one grants that increased knowledge is socially desirable, the investigator has to weigh a more complex set of considerations.

Elements of the Ethical Conflict

According to the preceding discussion, the ethical problems associated with psychological research on human beings cannot be solved by enunciating simple principles that point to absolute rights and wrongs. When ethical questions arise, the situation is usually one of weighing the advantages and disadvantages of conducting the research as planned. On the one hand, there is the contribution that the research may ultimately make to human welfare, on the other, there is the cost to the individual research participant. Put in these stark terms, the essential conflict is between the values of science to benefit all mankind and the values that dictate concern for the research participant.

Within this broad framework of competing values, there are more specific conflicts, often between positive values that we would all accept. For example, the obligation to obtain informed consent might require a researcher to tell participants that they had been selected for study because of evidence of strong but unrecognized homosexual tendencies. To provide participants with this information, however, would conflict with another obligation, to avoid treating them in ways that could be harmful or create stress. Consider another example: If an investigator learns in the course of a study that a particular research participant has serious emotional problems, confidentiality requires that this knowledge not be revealed to others; but a general concern for the individual's well-being may call for communicating the information to someone who could provide the necessary help.

In still other cases, the ethical desirability of using methods that will avoid misleading results may clash with ethical principles concerning desirable conduct toward research participants. One example of this type follows: According to the principle of informed consent, a research participant should be allowed to refuse to participate in a particular study, to withdraw at any time, or to accomplish the same result by having his data destroyed. If people who refuse to participate or withdraw their data are not a random sample of the relevant population, a biased sample results that may invalidate statistical tests or make generalizations misleading and violate the psychologist's obligation to do important and interpretable research.

Especially difficult problems of this type arise in research where some treatment of potential beneficial value is used. Good experimental design may require that persons in a control group be deprived of the treatment for the duration of the study; concern for the deprived individuals argues in the other direction.

Two General Considerations Regarding Research with Human Beings

These complexities form the background for two general considerations regarding ethical standards for psychological research with human beings. First, given the initial ethical obligation of the psychological scientist to conduct the best research of which he is capable, ethical conflict is sometimes unavoidable.

We therefore are concerned with conflict resolution, not with the advocacy of ethical absolutes. The general ethical question always is whether there is a negative effect upon the dignity and welfare of the participants that the importance of the research does not warrant. Second, in weighing the pros and cons of conducting research involving ethical questions, priority must be given to the research participant's welfare. The nearest that the principles in this document come to an immutable "thou shalt" or "thou shalt not" is in the insistence that the human participants emerge from their research experience unharmed—or at least that the risks are minimal, understood by the participants, and accepted as reasonable. If possible, participants should enjoy an identifiable benefit. In general, after research participation, the participants' feelings about the experience should be such that they would willingly take part in further research. The requirements of the research should be ones that research psychologists would find acceptable were members of their immediate families to participate.

Balancing Considerations For and Against Research That Raises Ethical Issues

Whether a particular piece of research is ethically reprehensible, acceptable, or praiseworthy—taking into account the entire context of relevant considerations—is a matter on which the individual investigator is obliged to come to a considered judgment in each case, without abdicating this responsibility on the grounds of current practice or judgment by others. In making this judgment, the investigator needs to take account of the potential benefits likely to flow from the research in conjunction with the possible costs, including those to the research participants, that the research procedures entail.

Such an approach does not lend itself to any quantitative formula or decision rule. Further, there remain difficult questions as to how costs to the individual participant can be balanced against possible ultimate benefits to science and to society, and as to who has a right to make such decisions. An analysis following this approach asks about any procedure, "Is it worth it, considering what is required of the research participant and other social costs, on the one hand, and the importance of the research, on the other?" Or, "Do the net gains of doing the research outweigh the net gains of not doing it?" The decision may rule against doing the research, or it may affirm the investigator's positive obligation to proceed. Such an analysis is also useful in making choices between alternative ways of doing research. For example, "Are the costs to research participants greater or less if they are informed or not informed about certain aspects of the research in advance?" "What will be the effect of these two alternatives on potential gains from the research?"

Suppose that an investigator has concluded that the effective study of a particular problem requires deception of the research participants. Among the possible costs or disadvantages of doing the research are that the deception may offend the participants or damage their self-esteem, give psychological research a bad name and work to the detriment of the research of others, lower the level of the participants' confidence in the quality of their relationships with others, or provide them with a bad example on which they may model their behavior. Among the possible advantages are the potential theoretical and social gains from the research, avoidance of misleading results should deception not be employed, and the research participants' opportunity to learn something about psychological research and have the satisfaction of contributing to the social benefits provided by the research.

Such a listing obviously does not provide an adequate basis for decision as to whether a given study should be conducted. We need to form a judgment about the likelihood and seriousness of the costs, the probability and importance of the gains, and the number of people who will be affected. Some factors we can assess objectively and reliably. For example, we can assure that the individual receives whatever was promised as payment for participation. We also know the number of participants to be exposed to whatever discomforts or indignities that the study may impose. We know also, however, that psychologists differ widely among themselves as to whether such experiences are felt by the research participants to be harmful, inconsequential, or positive. The same experience, for example, reaction to psychological stress, is judged by some to be potentially harmful and by others to provide a valuable opportunity for the development of self-understanding. Still others will say that the stress concocted by psychologists is so trivial compared to normal everyday stress experiences that research participants characteristically shrug it off as inconsequential. The theoretical and social gains from the research might conceivably be assumed to extend to all of society. Again, however, to estimate the probability or magnitude of such gains or the number of people affected is difficult, and judgments will vary greatly from one psychologist to another. Given the cumulative nature of science, the probability that the results of a single study will have any beneficial influence on society is very small, but, then, so is the probability that the research participant will view his experience in the research negatively. It is often possible, moreover, for the investigator to lower this probability. In the case of deception, for example, the chances that the research participant will be harmfully affected may be reduced to a minimum, if not eliminated entirely, by appropriate postexperimental information and interpretation. But, again, all of these judgments are subjective and lead to unavoidable difficulties in making ethical decisions.

Correcting the Investigator's Bias

The investigator should not trust his own objectivity in balancing the pros and cons of going ahead with research that raises an ethical question for him. His personal involvement tends to lead him to exaggerate the scientific merit of what he is about to do and to underestimate the costs to the research participant. In addition, he may be hindered from seeing costs from the latter's point of view, because of differences in age, economic and social background, intellectual orientation, and relationship to the project itself.

It is important to distinguish between costs as they appear to the investigator, as they would be consensually judged by colleagues, as members of the general public might see them, and as they are seen by the research participant. The gains anticipated from the research and benefits to be received by the participants should be appraised from each of these perspectives. The investigator must also recognize the possibility that both the benefits to the participants, and importantly, the costs of their participation in the research may vary from individual to individual. Where individual differences in reaction to research procedures can be consequential, the researcher is obliged to attempt to screen out of participation those for whom risks would be high.

Individual Responsibility and Collegial Review

The fact that the investigator cannot count on his own judgment to be unbiased underlies the recommendation that the investigator turn to the advice of others. But to whom should he turn for advice? It is often proposed that clergymen, lawyers, members of the laity (e.g., students) and, of course, other psychologists be used as advisors on the ethical acceptability of proposed research. Consensus on this matter has yet to develop.

A recommendation that the investigator seek the advice of others on ethical issues should not becloud the point that whatever the legal or administrative requirements for collegial review may be, the investigator may not delegate or evade the responsibility for the critical ethical decision which intrinsically rests with him. He should seek advice with respect to the potential costs of the research procedures to the participants, whether or not there is a legal requirement to do so. At the same time, however, he should understand that the advice received may be quite invalid, when it is permissive as well as when it is proscriptive. For this reason (as well as the commonly recognized scientific reasons) pilot studies are particularly valuable. In such preliminary work the investigator should obtain as much information as possible about the participants' reactions and, if the study is seen as painful, anxiety-provoking, dehumanizing, etc., attempts should be made to adjust the research procedures and increase the participants' benefits. Once more, however, the investigator must accept the final ethical responsibility as to how or whether to proceed. Collegial review, which can be perfunctory, should neither substitute for nor diffuse personal responsibility.

Note that the type of consultation under discussion focuses on ethical issues relating to the research participants. It does not involve a review of the technical questions of research design and analysis. Further, this type of consultation is to be distinguished from the review provided by institutional review committees. Such committees function primarily to maintain the ethical standards of the institution and to enforce the guidelines issued by funding agencies. They may, incidentally, advise the investigator about procedures. Typically, however, they are too overloaded to fulfill this function adequately.

Responsibility for Assistants

The ethical responsibility of the investigator entails certain additional obligations to others. Research is often conducted by assistants and technical personnel to allow scientists to devote their time to the work for which they are specially trained. Such research arrangements impose on the investigator the additional ethical responsibility of making sure that these assistants conduct the research as the investigator would. This requires instructing assistants (and indeed all his students) to be sensitive to ethical issues and, in addition, to provide them appropriate monitoring and supervision.

Differing Research Contexts That Affect the Judgment of Relative Gains and Costs

The foregoing discussion has implicitly assumed the context, typical of much basic research, in which neither the investigator nor the research participant expects the research experience to benefit the participant in other than educational and perhaps financial ways. This is of course by no means the only context of psychological research on human beings. Research is also conducted in service settings such as hospitals, where the participant expects important benefits. It is conducted in prisons and in military settings, where ordinary freedoms are substantially restricted, and in business and industry where the employees have obligations that follow from their employment. It is conducted with children (and other subjects who lack full adult competence) who are especially vulnerable and not fully capable of evaluating their own interests. And it is undertaken in cross-cultural settings, which involve special sensitivities and ethical responsibilities. The emphasis in the reported incidents that underlie the Principles and this discussion is on basic research in academic settings; to a lesser extent, on applied or basic research in clinical or educational settings. Because of this emphasis, the discussion of the application of the Principles to particular settings and categories of participants is not as balanced as one might wish.

Research conducted in the context of human services, for example, in clinical settings, encounters a matrix of potential costs and gains that differs substantially from that of basic research in academic settings. In part this is because both the participant and the investigator may expect the former to benefit significantly from participation.

An example will make clear the relevant difference between these contexts. When the research may be of direct benefit to patients who are research participants, the persons responsible for chronically psychotic adults or self-destructive autistic children may be willing to accept risks and costs of research that are appreciably greater than would be acceptable in the setting of basic research. In such a context, for example, the psychologist may responsibly regard the use of pain-producing aversive techniques as acceptable if in his judgment they offer the only chance of improving a severely debilitating and otherwise intractable condition of the research participant.

Among the considerations to be noted in the service-related context are the following: First, in a relationship defined primarily in terms of human service, research that is undertaken must be compatible with the underlying expectation of service. For example, research in a university counseling center requiring the participation of counseling center clients should involve the potential for improving the service program of the center. Hopefully, it will lead, in addition, to improving the quality of professional services provided to the research participants themselves.

Second, the strong motives inherent in the service relationship must not be exploited to the research participant's detriment. For example, the psychologist in a service context must be careful not to exercise undue coercion on the client, employee, patient, or student to participate in research by allowing the potential participant to draw incorrectly the inference that the service is contingent upon participation in the research. In situations in which services are contingent on research participation, that fact must be made explicit. In service-related research the value of seeking advice from colleagues and other advisors regarding ethical issues is especially great.

Still other contexts that affect the terms of ethical decision are those of research in business and industry and in military settings, where the structure of authority affects the meaning of voluntary consent.

The relatively brief discussions in Part II of special ethical considerations in research with children may be supplemented by reference to "Ethical Standards for Research with Children," nearing final formulation by the Society for Research in Child Development. A detailed treatment of "ethical considerations in the conduct of cross-cultural research" by the Subcommittee on Cross-Cultural Research of the APA Committee on International Relations in Psychology should also be available soon.

Ethical Issues Related to the Social Context of Psychological Research

This introductory survey of ethical complexities of psychological research on human beings makes clear how the growth of psychology has highlighted ethical issues that attracted little attention two decades ago. The urgency of present social problems and the social conflict and dissent that accompany them add to the pressures that the investigator has to take into account.

One group of issues that arise from the political-economic-social context of research relates to the sponsorship of research. Although such traditional sponsors as universities and hospitals continue to support research, other agencies have entered the picture: a dozen departments of the federal and even state governments, big business, political parties, and the communications media. It is understandable that these agencies and organizations support research in whole or in part as one means of furthering their institutional aims: To make peace or war, to increase profits, to appeal to the masses, to educate the citizenry or socialize its members or to elect a president. Every one of these goals (even that of socializing the individual) is potentially objectionable. May an ethically responsible research psychologist accept support from an organization with personally objectionable aims if he believes the research will have other beneficial effects?

Sometimes the sponsors of research offer support with strings attached, not allowing publication or permitting it only if the results come out a certain way. Given a scientific commitment to the free dissemination of knowledge, is it ethically permissible for an investigator to accept research funds under such restrictions?

Similar questions arise in connection with the involvement of certain populations in research. Under what conditions is it ethically acceptable to study residents of the ghetto, the intellectually handicapped, the poor, prisoners, or even college students? The researcher who undertakes to study these groups is sometimes charged with being opportunistic, exploitative, and potentially damaging to the target populations. The charge is made that, in the wrong hands, the results of research might easily be turned against the participants whose cooperation made them possible. What are the investigator's responsibilities toward such possible misuses of his work? And in circumstances of manifestly severe human need and acute but remediable human misery, is it acceptable and responsible to use for research purposes resources that could be applied to direct service? If so, under what conditions?

At this point in time, we are not yet ready as a profession to take a unified stand on the issues underlying such questions. We can only raise them and tentatively apply the approach of weighing pros and cons that has appeared fruitful elsewhere.

Consider, for example, the instance of the psychologist's obligation to publish research findings. If they have potential social value, this will be realized only if the research is published. Suppose the sponsor places restrictions upon the investigator's right to publish. How serious is the resulting ethical problem? Obviously, the answer depends upon the character of the research. If important findings are permanently withheld from publication, this is a failure to meet the highest scientific obligation. But the words "important" and "permanent" both need to be taken seriously. Too often in discussions of research we speak as if the enterprise consisted of a continuous parade of breakthroughs, day-by-day. Yet we know that this picture is misleading. Contributions come from the accumulation of evidence that finally shows that an effect is dependable and of wide applicability. So a situation that allows eventual publication may sometimes be more comfortable ethically than one that forces immediate commitment of research results to print.

Once published, data become public and the scientist *qua scientist* has no peculiar right to control their use. In any case, the investigator has no practical control over it—a consideration that may appropriately affect the initial decision as to what research to undertake. The guiding principles here involve personal values; one should take into consideration the prevailing moral standards and professional consensus but should not abdicate personal responsibility.

Indeed, what one investigator regards as misuse, another might take to be an application of the data in the service of the highest principles. It is also important to recognize that judgments of this type are not scientific judgments. They are social, political, economic, moral, esthetic, or something else. As a *citizen* the psychologist may feel obligated to participate in courses of action involving the use of scientific data, but the ethical considerations involved here lie outside the bounds of the scientific enterprise. In their capacity as research scientists, psychologists cannot reasonably be held to agree upon consensual standards in this respect.

There remains a serious and controversial issue to be noted. One frequently hears it asserted that behavioral research is contributing directly to the moral ills of society. According to this argument, when an investigator invades the privacy of another person, employs deceit, or occasions pain or stress, he contributes to legitimizing these indignities, and therefore to their prevalence in interpersonal behavior. Many psychologists discount such claims, noting that it is quite easy for a research participant to understand the reasons for these behaviors when they occur in a research context and to distinguish them from their counterparts in everyday life. Research is needed to help establish the factual basis for estimating ethical costs and gains of controversial research procedures in this respect as in others.

While we have no way of knowing whether behavioral research has in fact become an important causal factor in the current social malaise—the attrition of human relationships reflected in depersonalization and distrust with which many sensitive observers of the present-day human condition are concerned— we believe that psychologists would not accept the prospect that research in particular fields of psychology might become careless of human feelings and welfare. The aspiration of research psychologists, we believe, is to conduct their research activities in such a way as to reflect respect for the dignity of their human subjects and to take full responsibility for their welfare as research participants. As the ethical principles make clear, this goal has implications that begin with the decision to pursue a given study and conclude with steps to protect the confidentiality of research data. En route between these points one encounters the use of advisors on ethical issues, the obligation to obtain whenever possible the individual's informed and coercion-free consent to participate, fair and respectful treatment of the research participant in the course of the research, protection of the research participant from physical and mental stress, and removal of any stress produced by the research experience.

We may find it necessary upon occasion to ask our human research participants to suffer indignities in the service of developing a meaningful science of behavior. They will be likely to do so with understanding and endorsement provided that our own orientation reflects the respect and concern called for by the ethical principles that are set forth here.

III. COMMENTARY ON THE ETHICAL PRINCIPLES

The ethical principles for research involving human participants are necessarily phrased in general terms. Hence, questions will arise about their applicability to specific problems. The extended discussion that follows is designed to answer such questions or at least to raise the factors that should be considered in answering them.

A numbered section of the commentary is allocated to each principle. Exceptions to this occur in three instances in which a pair of related principles are covered in the same section. Where this occurs, the section has been given the numbers of both principles to facilitate locating the appropriate discussion material. Thus, Section 1-2 covers Principles 1 and 2.

Each section begins with a review of the problem or issue that gives rise to the need for a guiding principle. There follows a list of "incidents" or research descriptions which serve as concrete examples of the problem. Then, following a restatement of the principle, there comes a discussion relating the principle to various special problems, research settings, and populations of research participants.

Section 1-2. The Decision For or Against Conducting a Given Research Investigation

The basic problem faced by the investigator in planning research is how to design the study so as to maximize its theoretical and practical value while minimizing the costs and potential risks to the humans who participate in it. A particular study is ethically unacceptable to the extent that its theoretical or practical values are too limited to justify the impositions it makes on the participants or that scientifically acceptable alternative procedures have not been carefully considered.

There are a number of long-established and reasonably effective mechanisms for assuring the soundness of the psychologist's judgment concerning the best ways to maximize the basic and applied scientific values of his research. Graduate training programs in psychology, critical reviews of research reports by editorial consultants for journals and books, and evaluations of research proposals by panels of experts who advise funding agencies all help to educate the researcher in assessing whether the results of an investigation will have scientific or practical value—though the investigator should be aware that his personal investment in his own research ideas may lead him to exaggerate the potential contribution of his proposed study.

Less well developed, however, are professional mechanisms for assuring that the costs and risks to the human participants are accurately assessed and kept to a minimum. While the mechanisms for assessing scientific value are not indifferent to the costs of research to the participants, they have been more conspicuously concerned with assessing the scientific quality of the research. Only in recent years (and often only in response to student complaints or specific directives from federal agencies) have we seen the wide-spread establishment of a formal mechanism—the department "subject pool" committee or the institutional ethics review committee—dedicated primarily to safeguarding the welfare of human participants in research. Every study makes some impositions on the participants that, while typically quite minimal, may sometimes be appreciable. It is probably often the case that they are assessed as less serious by the investigator than by the participant or an outside observer.

The investigator, therefore, must ascertain whether it would be ethically responsible to conduct the research he has in mind when one takes participants' costs as well as scientific and social gains into account. Are the risks and costs to the participants so serious as to rule out the study, or to require its radical redesign, no matter how great its potential value? Or, does the research promise to contribute so much to psychological science or to society or even to the welfare of the participants themselves that it should be carried out even though it imposes great demands on them? Answering these questions involves facing complex issues. If the research is done, might it harm the participant or contribute to a social climate of manipulation, suspicion, and lack of trust? Is the development of a science of human behavior and experience so vital to the survival of our complex society that to fail to conduct the research is to abdicate one's basic obligation as a psychological scientist? Is the psychologist ever justified—and perhaps even obligated—to conduct research that exposes human participants to severe physical or mental stress?

These and many other questions must be considered by the investigator in the initial, fundamental decision to conduct, to modify, or even to abandon the research he has in mind. What are the possible gains from the research that its abandonment will forego, and what kind of impositions on the participants or on society might be made by carrying it out? How can the researcher check his own subjective and biased judgments in reaching a decision? When and where and on what issues should the researcher obtain advice in difficult situations? In collaborative research, where does the responsibility reside for making the decision to proceed or to abandon the research? The incidents below illustrate these issues, which are so fundamental and pervasive that most of the other incidents cited throughout this document are also relevant to them.

Incidents

1. I prepared a research proposal involving manipulation of level of initial self-esteem. The manipulation involved having some subjects experience failure in an interpersonal competition. Two persons of the same sex were to have competed for the attention of a member of the opposite sex with it pre-arranged for the one subject to experience an embarrasing defeat and another a satisfactory victory. There were grounds for thinking that, with my subjects, this would provide a far more effective induction of low (and high) self-esteem than, for example, competition in an intellectual task. I could think of no way of giving the subject advance warning without completely destroying the self-esteem effect.

2. Some years ago, I did research on *attitudes* toward cheating among college students. It would have been desirable, from the point of view of science, to go beyond anonymously expressed attitudes to related *behaviors*. One could observe cheating systematically, however, only by deceiving subjects. I could have used a technique such as returning already graded multiple-choice exams for (supposedly) self-grading and then counting answers that were changed by students during the grading. Such techniques seemed to me to raise very serious questions about relations between people (i.e., both the experimenter and the subject being considered simply as human beings), and more specifically, about professor/student relations. Was this my right as a scientist? What would happen to the classroom situation? I decided not to pursue the project in this direction, though assorted "rationalizations" (as I see them) were inviting; cheaters deserve to be found out, the others have no complaint. I discussed my problem with colleagues. Some thought that my reservations were ridiculous and not worth sacrificing a research project for. I am still convinced that the gains for psychology and human knowledge would not have been sufficient for me to have used the techniques I rejected.

3. I have conducted a number of participant-observation studies, in which the subjects were unaware that they were being observed. Each time I conduct such a study, the ethical problem arises concerning the very act of disguised participant observation. There is no doubt that such a field technique can yield data in natural settings which would be unattainable or seriously confounded if the subjects were aware of the presence of an active investigator. My resolution of the ethical problem of invasion of privacy, disguising one's true role, etc., essentially is based upon a rudimentary cost/benefit analysis. That is, I consider at length the value of the data sought, the possible effects of publication of the findings on the subjects, and the relative degree of privacy that actually is being violated. If I have serious misgivings about any of these factors, I will not conduct the research. Furthermore, once I have developed the experimental design, I solicit critiques from professional colleagues whom I consider to be sensitive to such issues, and incorporate their opinions into my final decisions about the research. Additionally, at the completion of a partici-pant-observation study, I reveal to the subjects that, in fact, I have been interested in the social-psychological processes manifested and hope to write

about them. I interview the subjects (most of these have been small group studies) and sound out the sensitivities of the subjects concerning analyses or interpretations I have made or will make. It has not yet occurred, but if the subjects strongly objected to the study or parts of the study, I would not publish the results.

4. A faculty member was doing research on techniques for reducing a snake phobia. Undergraduates were phoned by graduate students and told that they had to participate in the experiment. I am almost certain that the faculty member himself would not have taken this demanding stance, but he appeared to be lax in training and supervising his graduate assistants since they recruited subjects with such a disregard for informed consent.

Principles

Many of the research descriptions submitted by APA members bore on the researcher's decision for or against conducting a particular investigation on the basis of his weighing the scientific and social gains from proposed research against the anticipated impositions on the research participants. Some psychologists are inclined, at least on first consideration of the problem, to offer a simple absolute rule that one may never do research if it imposes some loss upon the participants. But further examination of the issue leads most people to a more complex judgment that there are matters of degree and circumstances that must be taken into consideration. Most human experiences and social interactions impose losses as well as gains upon the individuals involved, and research does not differ in this respect. Moreover, the decision not to act is itself an ethical choice that can be as morally reprehensible as deciding to act.

One must look more closely into the specifics of the situation and its complexities in drawing up ethical guidelines. One has to take into account the degrees of loss and gain and their likelihood. But such accounting involves extremely subjective judgments that are vulnerable to systematic biases. In order to reach a fair judgment in such cases, therefore, it is essential to employ certain procedural safeguards such as securing prior advice from sensitive consultants and obtaining the free and informed consent of the participant. But the researcher cannot abdicate or dilute his own final responsibility.

Principle 1. In planning a study the investigator has the personal responsibility to make a careful evaluation of its ethical acceptability, taking into account these Principles for research with human beings. To the extent that this appraisal, weighing scientific and humane values, suggests a deviation from any Principle, the investigator incurs an increasingly serious obligation to seek ethical advice and to observe more stringent safeguards to protect the rights of the human research participant.

The further question of locus of responsibility for deciding whether to undertake or abandon the research arises when several investigators are involved in the conduct of research (as co-investigator, or as senior investigator and assistant, or as teacher and student). Such collaborative situations multiply rather than divide the responsibility, so that each of the parties bears full responsibility. For example, both the principal investigator who designed the research and the assistant who conducts it are fully responsible for safeguarding the welfare of the participants.

Principle 2. Responsibility for the establishment and maintenance of acceptable ethical practice in research always remains with the individual investigator. The investigator is also responsible for the ethical treatment of research participants by collaborators, assistants, students, and employees, all of whom, however, incur parallel obligations.

Discussion

These principles assert the responsibility of the researcher for the welfare of the participants when he makes a decision to continue or to modify or abandon the research. They also imply the need to consider specific circumstances and take various safeguards in coming to a decision in each case. In this section attention is directed to considerations that bear on the decision.

A. Types of Benefits and Impositions That the Researcher Should Consider

Abandoning the research implies foregoing various benefits that people might have derived from it. These include indirect benefits to the general public or to particular subgroups that might have come from its advancement of basic knowledge, or direct benefits to these groups from its immediately applicable results. Included also are the benefits to the investigator due to the enhanced feeling of worth that comes from doing the research or from the advancement of his career. The potential participants themselves would forego various benefits they might have received such as financial payments, learning about themselves or about scientific research, or feelings of gratification for having contributed to the advancement of knowledge or the solution of social problems.

On the other hand, deciding to continue the research might impose a variety of costs, such as providing knowledge that might be misused, or wasting social and human resources. But the costs of greatest concern in this discussion are those that involve imposing upon the participants in the research. The research may expose them to physical or mental stress, violate their privacy, or weaken their sense of morality or trust in others.

The researcher has to weigh these many conflicting considerations of losses and gains, which vary both in likelihood of occurrence and in seriousness. The decision to proceed or to redesign or stop cannot be made on the basis of a formula. But the fact that these imponderables cannot be quantitatively and objectively assessed is no excuse for not taking them into consideration. The fact that the decision must be based on such complex factors, subjectively weighed and susceptible to bias, implies that the researcher should check it against the judgments of others. Most obviously, the investigator should consider the judgment of the participants themselves by conducting the research only if there are people who will give their free and informed consent to participate (see Sections 3-4 and 5). Furthermore, where substantial questions arise, the researcher should consult with a variety of thoughtful persons in making the decision to proceed with or abandon the research. In the section that follows, aspects of such consultation are discussed.

B.   *Consulting with Others to Assess the Ethical Acceptability of the Research*

When to obtain advice. While all research imposes some demands on participants, these are usually trivial and well understood by the person who agrees to participate—for example, it takes an hour or two and involves no more than answering some questions or performing a few simple tasks. No other risks, costs, or threats to his immediate or long-term interests are involved. Even the most concerned observers probably agree that in most of the research reported in behavioral science journals, appreciable impositions are not made upon the research participants.

But as investigators turn with increasing frequency to research on questions that have immediate relevance for personal and social problems, the studies are more likely to involve procedures which raise ethical questions—covert observation, studies of ethnic and other group differences, intervention research, the use of deception, the invasion of privacy, the induction of mental or physical stress, the administration of drugs, and other threats to the welfare and dignity of the participants. To the extent that such practices are involved in a proposed study, the costs to the participant become substantial. The investigator incurs a correspondingly greater obligation to consider alternative research approaches that impose smaller costs on the participant and to obtain the advice of others in evaluating the ethical acceptability of the planned research.

Why is advice of others needed? The persons who propose a study may weight its potential benefits more heavily than would less partial judges for a variety of reasons; for example, the researchers' wish to contribute to a science of psychology, to alleviate social and human problems, to support their own self-esteem, and to advance their professional careers.

These same factors, plus the differences between the investigators and the participants in age, economic and social background, and intellectual orientation, may hinder them from accurately assessing risks and costs from the participants' point of view. Research psychologists have an ethical obligation to recognize these potential influences upon their ethical judgments and to take steps to protect themselves from such influences by obtaining the advice of third parties who are concerned with the welfare of the participants as well as with research progress.

Advice concerning costs and risks to participants. Scientific colleagues will be helpful in assessing the potential costs or risks to the participants. But because they share many of the investigator's values and characteristics, as enumerated above, they tend to have come of the same biases, and these biases may lead them to minimize potential costs and risks to the participants. For this reason, whenever ethical issues are involved, it is important for the investigator to obtain additional consultation from persons other than scientific colleagues, who will adequately recognize and weigh impositions on the participants. The diversity of research contexts and the variety of potential costs and risks to the participants' welfare are so great that it would be inappropriate to specify any standard composition of an appropriate set of ethical advisors. Rather, the consultation that should be obtained in a given study depends upon the particular kind of cost or hazard involved in the research procedures and upon the participants to be employed. Professional colleagues with special expertise in personality and psychopathology, or about the participant population, may be helpful in assessing the consequences of the induction of psychological stress. Medical consultation may be mandatory where certain types of physical stress are involved. Members of the participants' significant groups, for example, college students, minority people, factory workers, etc., might be consulted about the effect on members of their group who are participating in the research.

The nature and amount of consultation are related to the extent of potential costs. The kind and amount of consultation and related precautions required of the investigator are directly related to the extent of the potential costs and risks to the participants. Similarly, the greater the disagreement among various consultants concerning the extent of the costs or risks, the more carefully and extensively one should seek additional consultation and consider alternative procedures. Thus, while for most studies the investigator may feel that the costs are so inconsequential that no outside advice whatever is needed, research that involves a variety of risks and makes extensive demands upon the participants requires extensive consultation with persons representing a variety of perspectives. In extreme cases, where the scientific or practical value of the study seems very high but the potential risks or costs to the participants are also disturbingly great, the investigator should not proceed without extensive consultation. Normally, extensive pilot work should precede large-scale studies. Such preliminary investigation provides a means of assessing costs and risks on a relatively small number of participants. Only if this preliminary work indicates that the costs and risks are acceptable should the investigator proceed with the study.

The following incident describes a proposed study in which the potential risks and costs to the participants were very high:

Researchers proposed doing a controlled study of the effects of protein deprivation on the cognitive development of children by withholding food from a random group of children while their siblings were provided protein-rich dietary supplements. This investigation was to be carried out in a number of different locations in Africa. A small number of us opposed the prosecution of any investigation of this kind, arguing that there were humanitarian objections to this sort of activity. In addition, we argued that the results could only be null or favorable (i.e., the effects of enriched protein diet would be independent of or positively associated with cognitive development) so there was little to be gained, scientifically, from the investigation. There was, moreover, the risk of permanent harm or (in some of the more severely food-short areas) death to participants. There is no adequate justification for the conduct of research which risks human life or potentiality when the results can only affirm a deleterious reaction. In this instance, there is considerable evidence on hand already to show that protein deprivation has serious physiological, emotional, and (presumably) intellectual consequences in the development of children.

Role of institutional committees in assuring ethical treatment of research participants. The voluntary and self-initiated consultation process that has just been discussed is quite independent of the mandatory review of an investigator's research proposal by any institutionally imposed review group, for example, a university or departmental committee on the use of human beings in research. The operation of such groups falls outside the limits of a discussion of individual research ethics insofar as they are established primarily to fulfill the *institution's* moral and legal responsibility to human participants in research.

The contributions as well as the limitations of institutional ethics committees are illustrated by the following incident:

We have a university-wide committee that must approve any research involving human subjects if it is supported by funds from one of the federal agencies. They do serve to screen out the more serious cases of subject mistreatment and to make researchers think more about subject welfare. But the committee membership is too diverse, so seldom does it happen that there is a member sufficiently knowledgeable about a given project to pick up subtle problems, and the members are too busy to give any advice back to investigators whose proposals involve minor ethics concerns.

From the point of view of the individual investigator, the function of the institutional review group often is *clearance* of research plans in contrast to *consultation* on ethical decisions. While the institutional committee may on occasion provide advice on ethical decisions, a single group cannot effectively serve the dual function of evaluator and consultant.

Alternative procedures for securing ethical advice. Given that his initial appraisal indicates that there are matters of ethical concern on which consultation seems advisable, what alternative procedures might the investigator follow in obtaining such advice? In the paragraphs above we have suggested the types of persons whose judgment might be solicited. Through what procedures might such advice be obtained?

Two broad alternatives suggest themselves: One is to seek the advice of individuals, the other is to work through an ethics advisory group. If the second alternative is chosen, it may be implemented in two ways: either (*a*) through an ad hoc group for the research in question or (*b*) through a continuing group set up either by a psychological organization (e.g., a psychology department) or by a group of investigators using related methods or studying related problems (e.g., a small group of experimental social psychologists).

There are advantages and disadvantages to all those alternatives. The time and trouble involved in seeking out consultants argues for the efficiency of a continuing group. So does the fact of carry-over of knowledge and familiarity of issues from one consultation to another.

On the side of consulting with individuals is the consideration of flexibility. The consultants thought to be most helpful for the research in question can be chosen with no need for explanations to other persons who might have been consulted on other occasions.

Ultimate responsibility remains with the investigator. Regardless of the kind or the amount of ethical advice obtained from others, the ultimate ethical responsibility for the decision to conduct or to abandon or modify the proposed research falls on the investigator. His decision may or may not coincide with the advice obtained from his consultants—he may proceed despite negative advice or he may modify or abandon the research in the face of approval and encouragement. It may be assumed that the suggestions made by the consultants will have a substantial influence on the researcher's decision, even though these suggestions in no way allow him to abdicate his responsibility for his decision.

C. Locus of Responsibility for the Participants' Welfare in Collaborative Research

Principle 2 states the ethical ideal for the not-infrequent situation where an investigator is engaged in research in collaboration with another. Included here are cases involving coprincipal investigators, or involving a senior researcher and an associate, assistant or employee, or involving a student and teacher in research assigned as part of an educational requirement. The principle states the demanding but unavoidable rule that responsibility can only be multiplied, never divided, by such collaboration. We examine below several aspects of ethical responsibility in collaborative research.

The principal investigator's responsibility. If a senior researcher designs the study but has the data collection carried out by collaborators, associates, student-apprentices, or employees, the senior researcher is as responsible for the humane treatment of the participants as if he himself collected the data. A principal investigator has the obligation to train assistants and students so that they will be ethically responsible, and must supervise them sufficiently to assure that the participants are being well treated. Graduate and undergraduate training in psychological research should be designed to assure that the students are as able and motivated to do research ethically as they are to do it skillfully. The need for such training is suggested by the following incident:

> Graduate students in a developmental course had to design their own experiment, develop procedures, and conduct the experiment outside of class at children's homes, where supervision was next to impossible. Each student was given a copy of the *Division 7 Code of Ethics for Research on Children,* and the entire class had to give approval to the proposed research before it was permitted. Occasionally students were talked out of a certain project by their peers (e.g., after the class discussion one graduate student dropped a project that would have involved encouraging elementary school children to cheat). Supervision of the actual conduct of the experiment remained lax because of almost insurmountable practical difficulties of supervising each student in the field.

Assistant's responsibility. The fact that, in such collaborative research efforts, the principal investigator or teacher retains responsibility for the humane treatment of the participants does not relieve the assistant or student of equal responsibility. That is, the student or assistant should be as sensitive to, and solicitous of, the welfare of the participants as if the research project were solely his own. It in no way excuses impositions on research participants to say that one was ordered to perform such actions by an employer or teacher. The following incident illustrates the problem:

Graduate student section leaders mentioned in class that all introductory psychology students were required to participate in a psychology experiment and that the course requirement would not be complete unless a student did so. They did not seem to be aware that they were employing an unacceptable degree of coercion until, after an undergraduate complained, a faculty member in charge of the course strongly and emphatically stated that this kind of coercion was not permissible.

Supervisor's responsibility to respect the moral judgments of assistants. The teacher or research supervisor should respect the moral judgment of students and assistants. Where they feel a moral reluctance to carry out a research procedure, the supervisor should not pressure them to do so, even though the procedure seems completely acceptable. A deviation from this practice is illustrated in the following incident:

Sometimes research assistants are coerced by faculty members to carry out research which offends their own sense of ethics. In our institution a visiting psychologist was doing a field experiment on prosocial behavior which involved a manipulation which most of the graduate students felt was dangerous and distasteful. Nevertheless, a number of graduate students were assigned to help this visitor carry out his research.

Section 3-4.   Obtaining Informed Consent to Participate
(Including Issues of Concealment and Deception)

They psychologist's ethical obligation to involve people as research participants only if they give their informed consent rests on well-established traditions of research ethics and on strong rational grounds. The individual's human right of free choice requires that the decision to participate be made in the light of adequate and accurate information. The fairness of the implied agreement between investigator and the research participant (Section 6, pp. 52–58) also rests upon the latter's informed consent.

Ethical problems arise because the requirements of effective psychological research often conflict with the simple fulfillment of this obligation to obtain informed consent. The relevant information may be too technical for the person to evaluate. In most tests of quantitative hypotheses, for example, the theory is beyond the research participant's comprehension. In the field of psychophysiology, the processes being studied may be completely unfamiliar to the participant. In many cases, the degree of discomfort or embarrassment to be experienced that would be relevant to the decision to participate may not be fully ascertainable prior to the conduct of the research. Certain classes of people (e.g., children, the mentally retarded, psychotics) may be incapable of responsible decision. By far the most common reason for limiting information, however, is that if the individual were to be fully informed about the purpose and procedures of the research and of the experiences to be anticipated, valid data could not be obtained. Methodological requirements of the research may demand that the participants remain unaware of the fact that they are being studied or of the hypotheses under investigation. Incomplete information or misinformation may have to be provided to elicit the behavior of a naive individual, or to create a psychological reality under conditions that permit valid inference.

These research requirements present the investigator with frequent ethical dilemmas. Under what circumstances, if any, is it acceptable to bypass, delay, or compromise acting on the obligation to give the person full information about the research and obtaining on this basis the required consent or refusal to participate? About what aspects of the research must information be provided? The issues that are involved here are closely entwined with ones subsequently examined in Section 5, Assuring Freedom from Coercion to Participate. They also touch upon considerations relating to the responsibility of the investigator to provide clarifying information at the end of a study (Section 8-9, pp. 75–87). This section provides a discussion of issues that center on the *informed* component of "informed consent"; the *consent* component appears in Section 5. Since deception, when it is employed in research, intrinsically compromises the information upon which consent is gained, it is considered here. It is to be noted, however, that, in addition, deception involves bad faith and thus raises a second and more serious ethical concern. For this reason, a separate principle is devoted to deception (Principle 4) rather than treating it entirely within the context of informed consent.

The range of problems arising in this broad category is suggested by the following incidents, selected from among the many submitted.

Incidents

1.   While the operational details of the experiment that affected him were explained to the subject, the basic purpose of the study was misrepresented by telling him that it was a test of the speed of the visual system, when it was actually a test of long-term memory. Telling the actual purpose of the experiment might have effected the subject's behavior and made the results difficult to generalize. In any case, the subject who was willing to take part for the stated purpose would probably be as willing to take part for the actual one.

2.   One of my doctoral students did an experiment designed to determine some correlates of the "cheating threshold" in college students. A test was administered, all test papers were collected and then photographed and returned. The students did not know that the papers had been photographed, and it was then made rather easy to change the answers on the exam so as to improve the score.

3.   Research on techniques for reducing racial and religious hostilities required participation of highly prejudiced subjects. The operational procedures were made clear to the subjects before they were asked to consent to participate, but neither before nor after the experiment was it disclosed to them that the

research was sponsored by an antiprejudice group or that the research was explicitly designed to study techniques for affecting racial attitudes.

4. A "notice of employment" was distributed. When the prospective "employees" arrived, however, they discovered that it was an experiment and not an employment interview. One subject had given up a half day of work and had had his suit cleaned; he felt he had been very badly treated.

Principles

From the introductory statement of the problem, and from the incidents just presented, it is clear that the ethical ideal of obtaining fully informed consent cannot be realized in much research without a serious risk that the results of the research will be deceptive or misleading. In addition, technical aspects of the research may exceed the limits of what participants can comprehend. Principles 3 and 4 are statements that may provide helpful guidelines to ethical behavior for the investigator who must cope with the complex problems of informed consent and deception.

Principle 3.   Ethical practice requires the investigator to inform the participant of all features of the research that reasonably might be expected to influence willingness to participate, and to explain all other aspects of the research about which the participant inquires. Failure to make full disclosure gives added emphasis to the investigator's responsibility to protect the welfare and dignity of the research participant.

Principle 4.   Openness and honesty are essential characteristics of the relationship between investigator and research participant. When the methodological requirements of a study necessitate concealment or deception, the investigator is required to ensure the participant's understanding of the reasons for this action and to restore the quality of the relationship with the investigator.

Discussion

Many kinds of considerations may be relevant to the potential participant's decision as to whether or not to participate in research. The purposes and sponsorship of the study may be a matter of concern. Just why *he* was selected to participate may be important. The procedures to be employed and the experiences to be expected are obviously relevant as are potentially beneficial or harmful aftereffects. There may be concern about possible uses to which the data or conclusions of the study may be put, as these bear upon the participant's interests and values or upon those of groups or institutions with which he is identified. Some of these complexities are inherent in the following incident:

During World War II we were doing research sponsored by the Air Force on training methods for pilots. We selected college students as candidates for training on the basis of a battery of tests, assigned them to training officers, and paid for their instruction. Some trainees were "washed out" on the basis of ratings made by the training officers. They experienced severe feelings of failure. In the course of the study we learned that the training officers were basing their ratings on very different criteria. This led us to develop a complex system of grading that took the trainee's performance and the trainer's criteria (both expressed as standard scores) into account.

Although this study seemed justified as a wartime project, I have often wondered if it would be ethical to do it today. How would college students react to the prospects of being subjects in an Air Force sponsored project? Would we have to identify the sponsor? Would we have to tell them that they were selected on the basis of certain tests? Would we be required to try to explain the system of evaluation? Would we have to tell them that there was a good chance they would fail and experience considerable stress? Just how much information may one withhold from subjects and still be ethical?

Providing complete information about all of the many conceivable considerations that might be important to any possible participant is obviously impracticable and would be unacceptable to the research participant and investigator alike. Human judgment is required as to what information the individual might reasonably want to have. Thus, it will often be desirable for the investigator's judgment in this respect to be corrected by consultation with others as well as by full responsiveness to the potential participant's questions about the research, whatever they may be.

Some people feel that respect for the dignity of the individual human being allows no compromise of the principle of informed consent. Others argue with equally deep conviction that society's interest in the advancement of scientific knowledge of human behavior will often justify some compromise of the ideal of providing complete information in advance. Principle 3 reminds the investigator of the responsibility to inform the research participant of every aspect of the research that relates to important values or that might otherwise affect willingness to participate. Where scientific considerations dictate the withholding of information, the ethically responsible investigator assumes personal responsibility for a careful weighing of the scientific requirements of the situation against the ethical requirements. The investigator should correct possible personal biases by seeking the advice of others, including persons with different value perspectives (Principle 1).

A.   *Involvement of Persons in Research without Their Knowledge or Consent*

In a special type of research situation, participants are unaware that they are participating in research, so that Principle 3 relating to informed consent must be regarded either as flagrantly violated or as in some sense not applying. The following incident provides an illustration:

I have conducted a number of participant-observation studies in which the subjects were unaware that they were being observed. There is no doubt that such a field technique can yield data in natural settings which would be unattainable or seriously confounded if the subjects were aware of the presence of an investigator.

The motivation to conceal from the person even the fact of participation in a research activity arises most frequently when the investigator feels such knowledge will influence behavior to such an extent that the research objectives cannot be reached. It seems impossible to study some phenomena if the individual is aware of the fact that a study is being made. This difficulty has led to concealment of research activity in a number of ways. These include covert observation and recording, disguised field experimentation, adding research manipulations to existing nonresearch operations, and obtaining information from third parties. The ethical problems raised by such concealment vary considerably in seriousness. They are discussed in the subsections that follow.

Covert or unobtrusive observation or recording of public behavior. In order to obtain direct, firsthand information uninfluenced by awareness of the data-collecting process, psychologists may wish to enter a natural situation under an assumed identity, or at least without revealing their research interests. In other cases, the effort to obtain records of natural behavior uninfluenced by the recording process has led investigators to use concealed recording procedures or devices to record aspects of behavior of persons who are not informed about the recording process, whether or not they realize that they are involved in research. Under what circumstances, if ever, is the investigator justified in adopting such procedures? The following incidents highlight some of the issues:

In a study of transportation patterns, a public agency copied down the license numbers of automobiles passing certain intersections, located the name and address of the car owner from official files, and sent a questionnaire asking how frequently and regularly this person passed this corner.

We do "unobtrusive" filming of shopper behavior in retail establishments. Some of these records are used for teaching purposes, some for research. In either case, before we show (or even *keep*) such filmed records, we request permission to do so from subjects. If refused, film is destroyed.

Recording complicates the matter, because the record is potentially permanent and poses a long-term threat to the privacy of the persons observed. It also adds to the problem of maintaining confidentiality (Section 10). The request for permission to keep or use the records, in the second incident, shows sensitivity to this issue; the linkage of observations with official files and direct questionnaire inquiry, in the first incident, raises more serious questions.

Whether or not there is recording, the involvement of the individuals concerned in this sort of research is minimal, and not to be compared with that of research participants in the usual sense. The experience of the "participants" is not affected by the research, and there are no direct positive or negative effects on them. The case approaches that of historical research (in which the public acts of persons are studied without their consent being thought at all necessary) or that of research with unobtrusive measures, where inferences are drawn from the "traces that people leave" without anyone's participating in the research at all.

In this connection it should be recognized that covert observation with hidden cameras or microphones is personally objectionable to many people, whether the observation is for research purposes or not. It is argued that such invasion of privacy could yield information that might be used against the observed individuals. Common acceptance of such practices might adversely affect attitudes of trust in interpersonal relationships. In terms of this argument, covert observation paves the road to the totalitarian society in which Big Brother is always watching. Whether or not such feelings are objectively warranted is beside the point. The feelings are real, and Principle 3 implies that they must be taken into account in the ethical analysis preceding the use of covert observation.

Covert or participant observation in private situations. Privacy is invaded by stealth, and the participants are allowed or enticed to make self-revelations that they might not make knowingly. Consider the following incident:

I worked for one semester on the production line of a large, nationally known manufacturing plant, and for a summer in another plant in a similar situation. My professional status (professor of psychology in a university in the city of location of the plants) was unknown to my co-workers. I was in the plant in the role of participant-observer collecting data on the human interaction, and for this purpose I kept very detailed daily logs via dictated recordings. Many of the findings proved later to be invaluable for teaching and research use. It was not until I was about to leave at the end of the period that I revealed my purposes and identity to the workers, some of whom I had become very close to.

The boundary between drawing legitimately on one's everyday experience and spying is a narrow one. Some critics feel that the investigator who invades private situations under false pretenses or with concealed observation is entirely out of bounds; others feel that there are problems and circumstances in regard to which it may be warranted. A widely publicized example that evoked both of these reactions concerned the study of homosexual behavior in public lavatories. In the role of "lookout," the researcher observed people in homosexual relationships, and then obtained additional information about the backgrounds of these individuals, all without informing them or revealing his own true identity.

The ethical investigator will assume responsibility for undertaking a study employing covert observation in private situations only after very careful consideration and consultation. Rigorous safeguards of confidentiality can mitigate, but do not eliminate, the ethical dilemma of an investigator whose scientific values encourage invading the privacy of others in this way.

Disguised field experimentation in public situations. The previous sections dealt with surreptitious research in which the investigator recorded a person's behavior without appreciably affecting his experience. In this section we are concerned with research in which the investigator not only records the unsuspecting individual's behavior but also covertly arranges or manipulates experiences. Encouragement from within the psychological profession and from the broader society to make psychological research more significant and more relevant to urgent social problems is increasing the frequency of this type of research. What is to be said about the ethical dilemma created by the accompanying increase in the frequency of deception? Some incidents will make the issue concrete:

One field experiment was planned, and another pilot tested, which involved the participation of subjects who were not aware that an experiment was in progress. In both studies the subjects were automobile dealers who were approached by trained experimental accomplices. In the planned experiment the subjects were used-car dealers, and the accomplice was to negotiate to sell his car for cash. In the pilot-tested experiment the subjects were new-car salesmen, and the accomplice negotiated to buy a car. There was never an intention, of course, either to buy or to sell, but just to negotiate. The purpose of the studies was to investigate the bargaining process as a function of the subject's perception of various characteristics of the accomplice.

In one study, two people gave contradictory information to a third person and argued loudly on the street over their disagreement. All three people were confederates of the experimenter. The genuine subjects were naive pedestrians in the vicinity. The question under investigation was "Under what condition will pedestrians gather to form a curiosity crowd?" A variety of social variables were manipulated. Following these manipulations and observations, subjects were surreptitiously interviewed for their "perceptions" of the staged events to ascertain the face validity of the manipulations; for example, a confederate of the experimenter asks a subject "What was going on over there (etc.)?" Subjects were never told that they were in an experiment.

When the man in the street becomes an unwitting participant in research, realism has been combined with experimental control, but sometimes at considerable ethical cost. Informed consent is impossible. In the least questionable cases, neither the anonymity nor the personal dignity of the participant is violated, and patience is only trivially imposed upon. But offenses to human dignity are readily imaginable in this sort of experimentation. As such procedures become more numerous in an effort to obtain information about important social issues, there is reason to fear their cumulative effect, which may tend to undermine mutual confidence in human relationships. Because of these ethical complexities and because of the investigator's own biases as an interested party, such research can be considered only with misgivings, for which the help of ethical consultants will be needed to resolve.

Adding research manipulations to existing nonresearch operations in institutional or action research. Often people are already in situations in which they are undergoing an experience that has nothing to do with research, and then a research aspect is superimposed (e.g., the relative merits of different textbooks are evaluated after they were already assigned within a school district; an ongoing therapeutic situation is observed to evaluate a therapist or a therapeutic method). In military research, different training methods may be compared; in industrial research, different job layouts or personnel practices; in educational research, different curricular approaches or teaching methods; in social-action research, different strategies of family income support. To the extent that the research aspect has little or no effect on what the participants actually experience, is it necessary to inform them of the research? How should we choose between the desirability of informing them and the probability that doing so will have behavioral effects that result in invalid inferences? Here are some representative incidents:

A high school reading test, felt to be in need of revision, was administered to pupils in several high schools during a regular class period with the cooperation of the schools but without voluntary consent of the pupils—since it was feared that making the participation voluntary would introduce selectional biases that would reduce the usefulness of the data. Unless this sort of thing is allowed, test development might be brought virtually to a standstill, but can pupils be required to participate when the purpose of the testing is more for the general improvement of the test instruments to benefit later students than the specific benefit of the pupils involved?

In an effort to test the efficacy of a creative sensitivity group experience in benefiting elementary school children with adjustment problems, a control group with equivalent problems was selected. Consent was asked from the children in the experimental group and their parents, but not for those in the control group, because no special treatments were given them and no special measures obtained from them directly. However, pre- and postteaching ratings were obtained on children in the control group as well as the experimental. Was it necessary to seek the permission of the control group children and their parents when the research so little affected their treatment?

The principle of informed consent would rule in each case that there is an obligation to inform the individual of his research role. Yet the importance of this information to the participant may be minimal, and there may be strong, countervailing, scientific and practical reasons for not providing it. Insofar as the research involves comparisons of reasonable variations in the normal program of institutions or agencies, there would seem to be no compelling case for insisting absolutely on the informed consent of the participants. Especially in industrial and military research, which occurs in settings in which participants may normally expect little freedom of choice, any such requirement would deviate sharply from currently accepted practice. Where special stress or risk is involved, or where the experimental variation otherwise exceeds "normal" bounds, the investigator is not absolved of ethical responsibility by any relationship to the institution or agency, however authoritative its charter may be. Whenever the participants lack the protection of voluntary consent, the investigator is under the special obligation to decide on the best grounds available, including the advice of others who are independently situated, whether the proposed procedures are ethically acceptable.

Obtaining information from third parties. Sometimes the only way to obtain the information needed for a particular study is to obtain it from the friends, teachers, acquaintances, counselors, or employers of the individual. The following incidents provide representative illustrations:

In a follow-up study of retarded adults discharged from institutions to independent community living, it was desirable to approach employers to determine the vocational adjustment of the subjects. Although the data obtained by direct contact with the retarded subjects were not as reliable, it was decided to avoid any contact with employers, neighbors, or relatives, because in certain cases the informant would have learned for the first time of the subject's retarded status and institutional history.

In following patients over an extended period of time, interviews are necessary with large numbers of people who may not be aware that the individual was a patient. To avoid causing the former patients embarrassment, interviews were restricted to individuals whom the staff knew to be aware of patient's status, or by getting patient's permission for interview.

These examples show that rather special problems related to informed consent arise when sensitive information is obtained from third parties. The procedure may reveal facts or presumptions about the research participant that the third-party respondent had not been aware of, and thus may violate Principle 10 relating to confidentiality.

Under ideal arrangements, the researcher should obtain from the individual being studied permission to approach others for the purpose of obtaining data. This may not be possible, however, when the individual cannot be located or for some reason is incompetent to give informed consent. In such cases the researcher should proceed only when a responsible analysis of the ethical situation and advice from consultants indicate that the interests of the individual are protected and that the scientific merit of the project is sufficient to warrant the ethical compromise. Having made this decision, the investigator then has the same obligations with respect to the third party as would otherwise pertain to the target individual. These include the obtaining of informed consent (Principle 3), and the maintenance of confidentiality (Principle 10) as perhaps the most important.

B.   A Note on "Invasion of Privacy"

The materials on covert observation and recording, and on obtaining information from third parties, discussed in the previous sections, touch upon the set of practices that many people object to as an invasion of privacy. It is to be noted, however, that invasion of privacy is a broader concept than informed consent as discussed above. For one thing it is not limited to research. The activities of criminal investigators, credit bureaus, and telephone salesmen are included, as are those of the psychologists who give tests for industry and the government. Researchers in the behavioral sciences seem far from the worst offenders.

A second point is that the critic who objects to invasion of privacy usually has in mind the surreptitious gathering of sensitive personal information about an individual. Secret filmings, recordings, tapped telephones, and opened mail are part of it; the open use of personality tests, opinion polls—even the national census—are another.

What is most objectionable in all of these cases is that people obtain information that is "none of their business." Objections to such invasions of privacy are greater if the information obtained then becomes in any sense public or if its collection puts the person under stress.

Because of the wide variety of issues associated with invasion of privacy, the materials in that area appear in several different sections of this report. Those related to informed consent have just been covered. Other important discussions of related materials appear in the sections on confidentiality (10, pp. 87–97) and psychological stress (7, pp. 58–75). There is no *one* principle against invasion of privacy but rather *several* that concern its various aspects.

C.   The Problem of Informed Consent from Those Not Competent to Give It

Legally as well as ethically, some potential participants in psychological research do not have the competence to give their informed consent. The problem arises with children and legal minors, with the mentally retarded, and with psychotics. Sound practice from a legal standpoint requires that the informed consent of the legal guardian be obtained for such an individual's research participation; the corresponding ethical consideration holds that free and informed consent should be obtained from a person whose primary interest is in the participant's welfare. The information needed for a decision in the participant's interest should be supplied.

But even in the case of legally incompetent persons, consent on the part of a parent or guardian does not obviate the need to provide information understandable to the potential participant whose wishes are to be respected. When a child, a mentally retarded person, or a disturbed patient is capable of making some reasonable judgment concerning the nature of the research and of participation in it, permission should be obtained from the participant as well as from the responsible adult or guardian.

D. *Deception*

The foregoing discussion has explored many aspects of concealment in research, from the standpoint of how it limits the informed consent of the participating individual and thus presents an ethical dilemma to the investigator who finds it scientifically desirable to employ it. The ethical problem here is simply that the research participant is *uninformed* with respect to one or more aspects of the research. Now we turn to the issues that arise when the participant is *misinformed*—when deception is employed with respect to the purposes of the study or the meaning of the participant's behavior. Two additional incidents will illustrate the problem:

College students were asked to volunteer for an experiment involving the evaluation of bets. They were told that they could choose a guaranteed $1.00 or, alternatively, the opportunity to participate in a gambling situation that could produce a maximum of $10.00 in winnings. They were told that their choices would be made at the first session of the experiment, and at a second session they could receive either the dollar or the opportunity to gamble. The second session was never held. Instead, subjects were given a sheet explaining that the deception had been necessary in order to obtain their cooperation, but that the experimenters did not have the funds to carry out their promise.

In a field study, some subgroups were exposed to right-wing party propaganda before their political attitudes were measured, with this material being presented in the guise of the interviewer's explaining how to fill out the questionnaire. To avoid revelation of the true nature of the experiment prematurely, and to avoid awkwardness, the subjects were not told the purpose of the experiment, nor was it revealed to them explicitly that they had been presented with right-wing propaganda under this guise.

The ethical issues raised in these incidents are more serious than those discussed so far, because the investigator has deliberately lied to the participant for scientific purposes. Thoughtful people who have considered the problem of deception differ sharply in their conclusions with respect to the use of deception in behavioral research. Many of them treat deception as a particularly serious instance of the more general problem of informed consent. For them, the issue is to be resolved by the same responsible weighing of scientific and ethical considerations as have been recommended in the preceding discussion. But others regard deception as an ethical issue of a qualitatively different kind. For persons of this view the maintenance of collaborative, open, honest relationships with other human beings and the avoidance of deceptive, manipulative ones is an ethical absolute. Nothing that threatens the personal integrity of the individual is ever acceptable, whether for research purposes or any other. Whatever position investigators take on the issue, it is their responsibility to take cognizance of the widespread objection to deception in any human interaction. To remind the investigator of this ethical necessity, the problem of deception has been made the particular focus of Principle 4.

The scientific purposes of research may invite the use of deception for a variety of reasons. Certain features of the research may be misrepresented because of the belief that an honest representation would adversely affect the potential participant's decision to participate. Having secured the participant's participation, it may be necessary to use deception to disguise the point behind a particular procedure or to conceal the meaning of the participant's reactions. Even at the end of the experiment it may seem better to leave the person misinformed than to reveal certain aspects of the study. In each of these cases, Principle 4 puts the investigator in a serious ethical dilemma: The research cannot continue without some compromise of this particular guideline.

Since the problem is so difficult, the investigator should seek advice before proceeding with a study that involves deception. Moreover, it seems advisable to consult with people whose values would tend to counteract one's own biases. Considerations that *may* make the use of deception more acceptable are the following: (*a*) The research problem is of great importance; (*b*) it may be demonstrated that the research objectives cannot be realized without deception; (*c*) there is sufficient reason for the concealment or misrepresentation that, on being fully informed later on (Principle 8), the research participant may be expected to find it reasonable, and to suffer no loss of confidence in the integrity of the investigator or of others involved; (*d*) the research participant is allowed to withdraw from the study at any time (Principle 5), and is free to withdraw the data when the concealment or misrepresentation is revealed (Principle 8); and (*e*) the investigator takes full responsibility for detecting and removing stressful aftereffects (Principle 9).

We turn now to the problems associated with the use of deception to secure participation and to achieve desired effects of certain experimental procedures. The discussion of one aspect of deception, its removal ("debriefing"), is postponed for discussion in a later section on the postexperimental treatment of research participants (Section 8-9).

Deception to obtain agreement to participate. Any investigator who is well acquainted with a research setting is aware of considerations that would lead potential research participants to refuse to cooperate. Thus there is a great temptation to employ misleading information in ways that get around the problem. The investigator may fail to mention that the study involves electric shock, that it requires a considerable commitment of time, or that it is sponsored by a controversial government agency; or false expectations about the events to be expected may be created. The following incidents provide examples:

An experimenter interested in creating realism in an experiment convinced subjects that they were being hired for a quasi-permanent job. At the end of one day of "employment," they were told that it was merely an experiment. One subject complained that he had turned down other employment opportunities on the strength of this offer.

We were interested in the effect of anxiety on problem solving in school, but since the word "anxiety" has threatening connotations to laymen, it seemed unlikely that we could obtain permission from parents to perform our experiment if we used that word when requesting their permission. Hence, we simply stated that each child would be given mathematics and reasoning tasks and that he would be asked to indicate on a "so-called" school anxiety questionnaire how he felt about solving problems in school. The quotation marks might have hidden our intention to use this test to obtain scores of both test anxiety and defensiveness.

These incidents illustrate some of the problems. In the first case, some people probably would have refused to participate had they not believed they had an opportunity for a long-range job; in the second, parents might have been reluctant to let their children participate had they realized the actual purpose of the study. The ethical burden on the investigator who decides to go ahead with research in either case is considerable, but no different in kind or mode of resolution from other dilemmas where important scientific values are in conflict with important human values. As in other such conflicts, the situation puts the investigator in the position of weighing the pros and cons of doing the study (or radically redesigning it), securing ethical guidance, and arriving at a difficult and ambiguous personal decision.

Deception as a part of the research procedure. In some research the provision of false information is intrinsic to the research design. Thus the following incident, representative of many:

In one study with male college freshmen, I returned false test scores to determine effects of success and failure on a subsequent task. Half the subjects were ranked in the top quarter and half in the bottom quarter. In the manipulation, I explained that the test rankings were highly correlated with IQ and probable grade-point average in college. After the second task I revealed the false scores and explained the purpose of the study. The fake test scores, the second task, and the explanation were in a single session so that any anxiety aroused by the manipulation would be quickly dissipated.

In addition to the deception issue, this incident raises the question of including mental stress (Section 7). With respect to deception, was this investigator in violation of Principle 4? From the information provided we cannot tell. But, referring back to our earlier general discussion, we can use the incident to provide a concrete illustration of the questions this experimenter should have asked himself before doing the study. In general, *Is this study important enough to warrant the use of deception, especially deception that results in stress?* A competent researcher can answer a part of the question by making sure that the answer to certain subsidiary questions is Yes—for example, is an important theoretical question at issue? Is the experimental design sound? Does the manipulation have the effect demanded by the problem under investigation? Will the research participant be allowed to discontinue participation at any time? To withdraw his data? Has the investigator the facilities needed to handle emotional reactions to stress should they arise? To assess the effect of the procedure upon the participants in the research, the investigator's unaided judgment is insufficient. Carefully evaluated information from pilot work on a few individuals should help, the investigator should also seek the advice of consultants, who might include representatives of the population from which the research participants are to come.

Given the lack of consensus on this issue among people of personal integrity, we cannot offer these procedures as clear-cut guidelines that would be accepted by all as a way of solving the ethical dilemma concerning the use of deception. They do suggest ways in which an investigator may face the issue squarely, and the types of advice to be sought from others. A major ethical concern remains, however, in the almost routine use of deception in certain areas of investigation. Serious attention to Principle 4 should make the employment of deception more the exception, less the rule.

Section 5.   Assuring Freedom from Coercion to Participate

This section deals with the extent to which it is ethically acceptable to bring pressure to bear upon people to participate in psychological research. The issue is complex and involves matters of philosophical importance. Complete freedom of choice is a cherished human ideal and coercion of any sort is an abridgment of that freedom. At the same time it must be recognized that hundreds of years of philosophical analysis of the problem under rubrics such as "free will" and "determinism" have neither completely clarified these concepts nor provided us with the necessary rules of ethical conduct. What does it mean to speak of the research participant's "freedom of choice" when one considers that such choices are the lawful psychological consequences of past and present influences in the environment? And how can we propose that a person deciding whether or not to participate in research should be free from coercion and at the same time maintain that all decisions are motivated and that they are affected by forces that act upon the decision maker?

Obviously the empirical materials that lie behind the discussion in these pages will not answer questions at such a basic philosophical level. What they can do, however, is to show two things: (a) that the problem of coercion in research with human beings arises in connection with a particular kind of influence—that which characterized situations where a person in a position of power uses that power to force another person to participate in research, and (b) that the exercise of such coercion varies a great deal in the extent to which it seems to exploit the research participant. Depending upon the circumstances, these instances range all the way from simple askings of favors to coercive demands that any observer would agree are unacceptable whatever his position on the more basic philosophical question.

The use of coercive measures to obtain the cooperation of participants in research is widespread. "Subject pools" consisting of all of the students enrolled in certain psychology courses exist in many universities. Employees in business and industry are required to participate in research under conditions where they might perceive refusal as placing their jobs in jeopardy. The participation of military personnel may be required under circumstances that virtually rule out resistance.

In instances that occupy extreme positions on a dimension of coerciveness, most observers would probably agree that the procedures used to secure consent to participate in research either are or are not ethically objectionable. For example, most people would probably agree that it would be unethical for an investigator doing research in a prison setting to force prisoners to submit to a highly dangerous research manipulation on the threat that failing to comply would put the prisoner's chance of being paroled in jeopardy. By contrast, almost no one would regard it as unethical to induce a college student to take part in a typical memory experiment by offering him payment for an hour's participation.

The worrisome examples fall between these extremes. To illustrate, even so conventional an incentive as money may become unduly coercive. A person in dire financial need, for example, the prisoner without money to buy cigarettes, might agree to participate in a hazardous experiment for a very small sum whereas others would ask a thousand times as much. In this case, is the exploitation of the prisoner's special situation not unethical? On the other hand, would it not be even more unethical to diminish the prisoner's freedom by withholding the opportunity? To consider another example, how coercive is it to threaten a patient with the denial of therapy for refusing to take part in an experimental study of the effectiveness of the therapeutic agent? Denial of a desperately needed service is generally seen as reprehensible but is there not something particularly appropriate in the case of the patient that warrants making research participation a condition of obtaining such a service?

So far we have mentioned only a few of the inducements that are used to motivate research participation. The range of such inducements is, of course, quite wide. Besides financial and other material rewards, moral appeals are used, such as promising the individual the satisfaction of knowing he has contributed to the advancement of science or to the solution of social problems, or that he has helped the researcher or some highly valued reference group. Or appeals are made on the basis of friendship, the positive value of cooperation, or the special needs of the investigator. Can this moral suasion ever become unduly coercive? To what extent is it permissible to use social pressure or statements that refusal to participate is a sign of uncooperativeness, lack of courage, and the like?

The problem of coercion sometimes arises even with persons who initially had no objection to taking part in the research. Having agreed to participate they may find the procedures painful, threatening, or more boring or time consuming than anticipated. Presumably freedom from undue pressure to participate should not end at the start of the experiment. Does a research participant surrender freedom of choice after deciding to participate or does such freedom continue to exist in the form of the option to drop out of the research at any point? Is the researcher ever permitted to impose a penalty for dropping out? If the person does not complete his participation, may the investigator withhold all or part of the promised payment? How far is the researcher obliged to go in repeatedly bringing the opportunity to drop out to the participant's attention? To what extent and by what means might it be permissible to urge a reluctant participant to continue because, for example, allowing participants to drop out may bias the data?

A few incidents will concretize several of the problems that arise in defining the investigator's obligation to assure that people who participate in research do so free from undue coercion.

Incidents

1. Because we felt uncertain about the ethics of requiring students to participate in research, they were given the option of participating in an experiment or reading a rather short, simple book on experimental procedures and then taking a very simple test on it. In addition, there were many different experiments from which students could choose. To make each experiment a learning experience for the student, we required the experimenter to discuss the experiment with his subjects, including stating as far as possible the purpose, design, etc.

2. Kidney patients were studied for intellectual changes before and after hemodialysis to investigate the possibility that uremia has subtle effects on cognition. The patient and his nearest relative were both asked to give consent. Nevertheless, there was some question about the reality of the voluntary consent in this case, where the patient's only hope of living depended upon acceptance and continuation on the program. Can this in any sense be considered a real choice?

3. Financial rewards were used with the destitute or with impoverished prisoners, to have them participate in research involving drugs or high-stress conditions where it seemed likely that persons under ordinary circumstances would not participate even for a considerably larger financial inducement. One worries that the researcher was taking advantage of people whose need is so great that they are hardly free to refuse in the usual sense.

4. We were studying the use of a new psychological test with psychiatric inpatients, and tried to get as complete as possible a sample by urging the patients to participate while not insisting on it. Part way through the brief testing, an occasional patient expressed a wish to leave the situation. In these cases, they were strongly reassured and encouraged to persist. Where was the line between reasoning and coercion under these circumstances?

Principle

Freedom of choice is a human value in its own right. It is particularly important in research because of its relationship to other ethical problems discussed elsewhere in this document. The need for freedom from coercion becomes increasingly pronounced to the extent that research participation entails risks or costs of any type to the participant. The following principle attempts to capture this ideal and, at the same time, to recognize the complexities that are discussed further in sections to follow.

Principle 5.   Ethical research practice requires the investigator to respect the individual's freedom to decline to participate in research or to discontinue participation at any time. The obligation to protect this freedom requires special vigilance when the investigator is in a position of power over the participant. The decision to limit this freedom increases the investigator's responsibility to protect the participant's dignity and welfare.

Discussion

In introducing the problem of freedom from coercion difficult questions were raised about a variety of issues that occur in interpreting the investigator's obligation to respect the individual's freedom to decide whether or not to participate in research. Here we shall give some indications as to how these questions might be answered in concrete situations by discussing further some special situations and problems.

A. *Recruiting College Students as Research Participants in Connection with Their Enrollment in Courses: The "Subject Pool"*

Problems arise in connection with the recruitment of college students to participate when such participation is required as a condition of enrolling in a course. This is the problem of the so-called "subject pool."

The topic is one on which there is a wide variety of ethical opinion. Not only do psychologists differ in their conclusions, but individual comments reflect ambivalence. The incidents often begin with an expression such as: "Because we felt uncertain about the ethics of requiring students to participate in research, we . . . ." Obviously there are arguments pro and con for such requirements, and both sides of the argument deserve consideration. The research participation requirement presents an ethical problem only insofar as it is imposed for reasons over and above the educational needs of the students. No ethical question arises when an instructor requires participation in research for valid educational purposes.

Arguments against the course requirement to participate in research. Those who characterize the requirement of research participation as ethically troublesome present one major consideration and several subsidiary points. The major objection is based upon an apparent inconsistency between the research participation requirement and the principle that research participation should be free of coercion. More specifically, it seems unduly coercive for a person in power, for example, a teacher, to require another person over whom he has power to participate in research as a condition of undertaking some line of action or receiving a service, for example, enrolling in a course. Supporting, but less central, arguments against the requirement include the following:

(a) The research carried out with undergraduate students as participants is seldom worth the cost to them. Being based upon a highly selected and over-studied sample, it cannot have much generality; the problems investigated are seldom of real consequence. (b) Although alternatives to research participation are routinely provided as ways of satisfying the requirement, these alternatives are often more onerous than participating in research, and they are seldom presented as real alternatives. The result is that students are actually coerced into participation. (c) In practice, researchers do very little to make the experience educationally or otherwise profitable to the participants. (d) To the extent that students see their participation as coerced, they can be expected to react in various negative ways that diminish the value of the research. (e) Such coercion is detrimental to more important aspects of the student–teacher relationship and to the free spirit that is central to the concept of university research itself.

Arguments for the requirement. The arguments on the other side touch on many of the same points but reach opposite conclusions. As regards the exercise of power over a captive student population, these psychologists ask:

Why single out research participation as a peculiarly blameful requirement? The teacher uses his position of authority every time he makes an assignment, schedules an examination or includes preplanned laboratory exercises as a part of the course. Why should the research participation requirement be viewed as less ethical than any of these?

In passing we should mention that this does not appear to be a valid argument although it occurs with some frequency. Assignments, examinations, and laboratory exercises contribute to the educational process in a way that the research participation requirement *may* not. An important component of a set of recommendations to be made later will be a description of procedures that help to guarantee an educational benefit when the research participation requirement is used.

Another argument that is frequently offered for the research participation requirement is that participation in ongoing research provides a more realistic and valuable educational experience than taking part in laboratory experiments especially arranged for training purposes: The latter tend to be artificial or trivial, and may be impractical given the large enrollments in many university courses.

Still another, and quite different, justification suggested for requiring research participation is that teachers of psychology have the right to require psychology students to make a contribution to the advancement of the science they are studying. Those who take this position note that the availability of research participants is a requirement if behavioral science is to advance. Students of psychology profit from contributions of time and effort made by research participants who have preceded them, it is argued, so it is right to expect them to make a parallel contribution to those who study psychology in the future.

This last point brings us to the heart of the argument presented in favor of the research participation requirement. If this source of participants did not exist, recruitment of people to serve in research would become much more difficult and often prohibitively expensive. Some potentially valuable research would not get done. Also, the participants who would remain available as volunteers for research would be self-selected, introducing probable biases in the conclusions drawn from research. As all of this suggests, this second position depends in an important way upon the assumption that research is a function of the university that is at least as important as its educational function.

Evaluation of the argument. The arguments just summarized are opinions that one hears advanced with great intensity. They derive from differences in the ordering of values. It is *not* that the attitudes of those who object to the research requirement are diametrically opposed to those who favor it, or that they relate directly to a "scientist–humanist" division in the field. In fact, as one of the incidents above demonstrated, "scientifically" oriented animal psychologists frequently oppose the requirement while many "humanistically" oriented clinicians favor it. What seems more central to the dispute is a matter of important self-interest deriving from the problems certain investigators wish to study. For those who study normal behavior in human beings, the availability of a group of human participants is essential. Their research and everything that hinges on it—the progress of their particular segment of behavioral science as well as their own professional status—is at stake. To these investigators the "subject pool" is as important as the library, the computing center, the clinic, the animal colony, or the community are to investigators with other specialized interests.

For reasons that will now be apparent, many researchers would regard it as highly improper for anyone else to limit their right to recruit students from their classes as research participants. They would view this as an interference with their efforts to fulfill the first and most important ethical obligation of the researcher—to conduct meaningful research. They would feel that the spirit of Principle 5 can be maintained and the recruitment of students to serve as research participants continued if the recruitment procedure preserves a substantial amount of free choice and otherwise protects the participants from undue coercion. When these precautions are combined with procedures that assure an educational benefit to the participant, the demands of Principle 5 appear to be satisfied. For this reason a number of university psychology departments have developed detailed procedures to guarantee the accomplishment of educational objectives and to minimize the element of coercion. Some of them are described in the next section. The account that follows is intended to be suggestive, not prescriptive.

Implementation of the research participation requirement. The procedures existing to protect the rights of human research participants differ considerably from one academic setting to another. A set of suggested procedures that includes the best features of several plans contains the following components:

1. Students are informed about the research requirement before they enroll in the course typically by an announcement in an official listing of courses. In addition, during the first class meeting, a detailed description of the requirement, frequently in written form, is provided covering the following points: the amount of participation required; the available alternatives to actual

research participation; in a general way, the kinds of studies among which the student can choose; the right of the student to drop out of a given research project at any time without penalty; any penalties to be imposed for failure to complete the requirement or for nonappearance after agreeing to take part; the benefits to the student to be gained from participation; the obligation of the researcher to provide the student with an explanation of the research; the obligation of the researcher to treat the participant with respect and dignity; the procedures to be followed if the student is mistreated in any way; and an explanation of the scientific purposes of the research carried on in the departmental laboratories.

2.   Prior approval of research proposals is required, sometimes by a single faculty member but more often by a departmental committee, that takes into account many of the considerations presented below:

Will physical or mental stress be employed? If so, what precautions have been taken to protect the participants from the possibly damaging effects of the procedure? Will the research involve withholding information or deception? If so, what plans have been developed for subsequently informing the participants? What plans have been made for providing the participants with an explanation of the study? In general, what will the participants gain? Have the procedures been evaluated by representative participants in a pilot study?

3.   Two types of alternatives are commonly available to increase the student's freedom of choice in meeting the requirement:

A variety of opportunities for research participation is provided. This lets the student choose the type of research experience and (often of more consequence to him) the time and place where he will participate.

Options are provided that do not require service as a research participant. The student may submit a short paper based upon the reading of research reports or observe ongoing research and prepare a report based upon this experience.

4.   Before beginning his participation, the student receives a description of the procedures to be employed and is reminded of his option to drop out without penalty later on if he so desires. At this point some investigators have the student sign a form indicating informed consent.

5.   Steps are taken to insure that the student is treated with respect and courtesy. The concept that the participant is a "colleague in research" is widely accepted. In the service of this concept, the term "subject" has been abandoned in some universities and the expression "research participant" has replaced it.

6.   Participants receive some kind of reward for their participation. At a minimum this involves as full an explanation of the purposes of the research as is possible. In addition, some departments still reward research participation with better grades although many critics would question the educational propriety of this practice. The assignment of a grade of "incomplete" as a sanction against nonfulfillment is common, although some regard this as too coercive. Where this sanction is used, procedures exist for allowing the student to fulfill the requirement later on.

7.   There is a mechanism by which students may report any mistreatment. Usually this involves reporting questionable conduct on the part of a researcher to the instructor, the departmental ethics committee, or the chairman of the department.

8.   The recruiting procedure is under constant review. Assessments of student attitudes toward the requirement are obtained at the end of each course having such a requirement each time it is offered. These data, together with evaluations of the workability of the procedures by the researchers, provide the basis for modifying the procedures in subsequent years.

Conclusion. The discussion above applies only to the use of a research participation requirement for recruitment in studies which, although primarily nonpedagogical in character, do offer the participant a potential educational gain. When, as is sometimes the case, the latter feature is missing, the investigator should consider the possibility of using other means of recruiting research participants. The ethical sense of this point is widely recognized. In studies that require many hours of participation the educational gain to the study is often exhausted early in the investigation. In such cases, it is common practice to pay the participants for their services. In universities where the medical school is on the same campus as the department requiring research participation, service in medical studies is sometimes specifically ruled out as a way of fulfilling the requirement, sometimes because of pedagogical irrelevance, sometimes because of problems of adequate screening of such studies in terms of ethical criteria. Where educational gains are available to the student, procedures like those discussed here do much to assure compliance with Principle 5 and the other principles set forth in this document for the purpose of protecting the welfare of human participants in research.

B.   *Recruiting Research Participants in Institutional, Industrial, and Military Settings*

The greatest compromises with the ideal of free consent probably occur in military, therapeutic, correctional, and business or industrial settings. In such settings research is incidental to the main institutional activity which in turn may be organized in ways that tend to minimize individual freedom of action. Perhaps, because of this orienation, relatively few incidents were submitted regarding the ethical problems of manifest coercion in these settings. The generally coercive character of such institutions may diminish the salience of the more specifically coercive aspect of research participation. Yet research goes on in these settings, and ethical questions arise because patients, prisoners, soldiers, and employees may be required to participate in research without a realistic option to refuse. Consider, for example, the following incidents.

We were comparing several innovative treatment groups in a mental hospital program. The patients were vocal, young men who were quick to ask if the program was voluntary. When it became apparent that the study would not be possible if it were set up as voluntary, we decided that all patients would be required to participate. Each would have to meet with his assigned group for the 15-minute sessions that were involved. Several patients expressed resentment, but we made it clear that repeated absences would result in return to the locked ward. Refusal to participate would mean that the patient would have to leave the innovative program. He would be transferred and would have to leave his friends and ongoing treatment programs, to rejoin a more chronic group of older men who were receiving much less treatment. We felt this was justified since the treatment groups were thought to be therapeutic, but the decision to participate was certainly not voluntary.

Workers in an industrial setting were assigned or asked by their supervisors to participate in research. While they were not required to participate if they showed any reluctance, I worried that under the circumstances they might have perceived the request as another job assignment which they were obliged to undertake if they did not wish to lose their jobs or at least incur the disapproval of their supervisors.

Some years ago (not long after World War II) we were doing research on problems of training under an Air Force grant, and we did our experimentation at major Air Force bases. In the typical experimental session, enlisted men were marched in by a sergeant, a platoon at a time, and were run through the experimental procedure without any explanation or justification for their participation. Although this was a way to collect a great volume of data rapidly, in retrospect I have often wondered whether we were in a defensible ethical position when we did this work.

We used prison inmates in a number of research projects and always asked for their consent. However, in retrospect, it seems to me that since I also sat on boards that made recommendations for parole and had other important influences on their prison lives, it might be questioned whether they really felt free to refuse in view of their high need in these areas.

How does Principle 5 apply in these instances? Are the ethical rules governing incentives to participate independent of time and place or does the institutional setting affect what pressures are permissible? For example, in military or industrial situations, are persons' expectations so different from what they are in academic settings or public places that pressures to participate may be used in the former that would be inadmissible in the latter? When research is conducted without the full voluntary consent of the participants, the decision to do so is commonly justified in terms of the value of the research to institutional objectives. Thus, in the military context, it is argued that soldiers may be expected to cooperate in research aimed at the development of a more effective army; in industry, that workers can be required as part of their jobs to participate in research toward the improvement of productive efficiency; in mental hospitals, that patients should be willing to participate in studies to produce better forms of therapy.

From the perspective of the research participant, however, the goals of the institution may be irrelevant or even objectionable. Many drafted soldiers may have no desire at all to further the objectives of the military. The patient may be afraid of the new therapeutic procedure to be tested in the research. The worker may believe that research in productivity lays the foundation for the greater exploitation of his group. How are the different views of the individual and the organization to be balanced in situations such as these?

In considering this question it is helpful to distinguish among three broad types of research occuring in the situations in question. The first is the type in which some aspect of the program of the institution or organization is being evaluated in the hope of improving its effectiveness. This is illustrated by the therapy experiment described in the first of the four incidents above. The second type is that in which the research is inherently related to, and hence must be done with, the particular type of person in the given setting—but may or may not affect his welfare or that of others like him. The research on intellectual changes in kidney disease, cited under Incidents (p. 41), illustrates this type. The third type is research that takes advantage of the availability of persons who are in the setting, for example, prisoners, but which is no more related to the activities, concerns, or disabilities of these persons than it is to those of people outside the setting.

The first of these three types of research presents the fewest problems. As already noted in Section 3-4A (p. 30), research participation that is incidental to systematic study of the effects of normal variations in a regular institutional program appears not to raise serious ethical concerns even when the principle of informed consent is compromised. Thus, just as the effectiveness of alternative curricula may legitimately be studied in educational research without explicit informed permission of students and their parents (other safeguards being observed), so may different policies of ward management be compared. The ethical compromise is similar in the two cases, and, to many, will seem clearly warranted. The safeguards of ethical consultation to protect the interests of the participants obviously become especially important when such a compromise is made. This consideration seems particularly important when major departures from standard programs are employed. In these cases the participant is in danger of being handled in a way that will interfere with improvement or rehabilitation. In such cases the researcher incurs a special responsibility to assure the later provision of such benefits as the research participant may have been deprived of in the course of the research (Principle 9). The coercive implications of the power relations between participant and staff in these settings is a further reason for exceptional care in protecting the participants' interests.

The second of the three types of research, that requiring the participation of persons like those found in a given institutional or organizational setting, raises issues that are harder to resolve. Viewed from the perspective of the staff research psychologist in, for example, a prison or a mental hospital, we recognize the obligation such a person feels to advance knowledge as it applies to the treatment of persons like those in the institution in which he works. It is easy to understand that this sense of obligation will enter into the investigator's own accounting of the costs and benefits of the research being considered. It is not surprising that such an investigator feels more free than one otherwise might to use strong incentives to induce potential participants to take part in the research.

A stronger way to put this last point is that prisoners and mental patients may ethically be required to cooperate in therapeutic or corrective programs oriented toward their own rehabilitation. By extension, this argument would hold that cooperation in research toward the improvement of rehabilitation might also be required of them. A difficulty with this position is that it is too readily available as a rationalization for exploitation. On occasion, the institutions in question may serve more to incarcerate and punish than to rehabilitate. Under such circumstances the argument just presented loses much of its force.

Viewed from the perspective of the nature of the institutions and organizations under discussion, a somewhat similar view of the ethical dilemma emerges. In varying degrees, the correctional institution, the mental hospital, places of employment, and the military all present situations in which people's customary freedom are restricted in various ways. Although people may have entered mental-hospital and military settings voluntarily, their conduct within these institutions is typically governed by many more rules and regulations than apply to the public at large. Employees in business and industry, moreover, agree to take considerable direction from their employers and supervisors as a condition of their employment. These restrictive features give rise to recurring issues of the human rights of prisoners, patients, draftees, or employees that society has not fully resolved—issues that clearly are involved when research participation is institutionally expected. In brief, socially important objectives in these cases sometimes seem to justify coercion and the organization of the institutions involved makes coercion easy. But these considerations often clash with the motives of the potential participant.

Awareness of the justifications and situational factors just discussed is a first step in protecting oneself against recruiting practices that show less than full respect for the dignity of the potential research participant. It is sometimes difficult to remember that a person who, from the investigator's point of view or the institutional point of view, *should* cooperate in research for which he is needed may feel no such obligation. To the contrary, as noted on page 39, he may even see the proposed research as operating to his disadvantage, for example, causing him discomfort, reducing his privileges, taking his time, etc. Such considerations raise serious questions about the use of altruistic or public service incentives in recruiting participants for such research.

Granted that we have here a real conflict between the pros and cons of using altruistic or public service incentives in recruiting research participants, can any suggestions be offered to deal with the dilemma? From one point of view we should recall that, according to Principle 5, the investigator must respect the potential participants' freedom to decline participation. Moreover, as Principle 5 also says, the investigator's position of power with respect to the participant obligates him to take special care to protect that freedom. This clearly rules out the commandeering of research participants described in some of the incidents.

From another point of view, however, Principle 5 does not imply that the investigator may not communicate to the potential participant his sense of the possible value of the proposed research and the need, as he sees it, for cooperation from individuals of the type represented by the potential participant. For the investigator to do this with conviction without at the same time bringing to bear the power associated with his staff position admittedly will be difficult. What must be attempted is to provide the potential participant with a meaningful argument that his participation may help solve a serious problem without at the same time implying disapproval or punishment for refusal to take part.

In the third type of research, that without any special relationship either to the program in the special setting or to the characteristics of persons in that setting, the ethical dilemma takes a different form. In such research the argument that the potential participant is under some obligation to take part can no longer be made. Accordingly, the focus shifts to the kind and strength of incentives the investigator is warranted in using. Many investigators have voiced concern with the special significance that financial incentives, staff approval and disapproval, etc., have to institutionalized individuals. Some of this concern was discussed previously on pages 39–40. In the research descriptions that investigators supplied, there is much testimony to the temptation to take advantage of the disadvantaged circumstances of potential participants in recruiting their collaboration. One precaution may be strongly recommended: when potential research participants have such strong needs that they have little real freedom to reject incentives related to these needs, an investigator should never use such incentives without first securing ethical advice from consultants.

C.   Clarity of the Person's Right to Refuse Participation or to Drop Out

Questions often arise as to whether the person's opportunity to refuse to participate or to drop out after he has begun participation is made sufficiently clear to him. Special problems arise when the demand characteristics of a situation are such as to make refusal or dropping out difficult. Other questions arise in connection with certain types of people or with certain states of mind. Whatever the circumstances, the conflict of the investigator derives from the fact that refusal to participate or dropping out diminishes the representativeness of the sample of research participants. To what extent should the investigator allow such considerations to lead him to limit these options? Some additional incidents will illustrate this problem:

Freshmen at an orientation procedure spent several days of hectic activity including diagnostic testing and the like. Intermingled in this testing material were some research questionnaires that were administered because of a longitudinal study on the effect of institutional attendance on personality and values. Just before they started to complete this questionnaire, they were told that it was not a required test; but there is some question as to whether under the rushed circumstances they had a meaningful opportunity to refuse participation.

We were studying psychological effects of tranquilizers, within the clinical range, on chronic schizophrenics in the research ward of a state hospital. In the middle of the experiment, one of the subjects said he had found out that participation was voluntary and that he wished to quit because he did not want to take the drugs or perform on the tests. I managed to talk him into staying in the experiment, without threatening him. However, I worried whether I might have used implicit threats since I was very anxious for him to continue, as it was my PhD dissertation.

For these cases it seems quite clear that the researcher could have given the participants a more explicit statement of their right to refuse to take part or to drop out of the study. The question of whether they *should* have leads to some interesting points. The contrast between the two examples suggests that the seriousness of the ethical problem depends a great deal upon the type of procedure being employed. With normal persons and a relatively minor imposition, the first incident raises only minor ethical issues. The second, using drugs, raises issues that are more serious. Here, pressure upon the participant to remain in the study is harder to justify and would require that a more substantial gain from the research be anticipated.

Special problems arise concerning the clarity of the person's right to refuse participation when the individual is in a special relationship of dependency with the researcher that might interfere with the exercising of the right to refuse. The teacher–student, doctor–patient, and employer–employee relationships are examples. One possible resolution to many problems of this type is to take special pains to protect the prospective participant's right to refuse by turning over the recruitment of participants and the conduct of the research to some third party not involved in the special relationship. Such precautions should help to protect the person's right both to refuse to participate and to drop out later on. In general, when the person has strong reasons to refuse to participate, there remains a coercive element, and the investigator is obliged to take correspondingly scrupulous precautions to assure that the research is warranted and that the participant's interests are protected. This kind of problem is considered further in Section 6 dealing with fairness and freedom from exploitation in the research relationship.

D. *The Participant's Right to Withdraw His Data*

Although Principle 5 does not specifically mention the right of the participant to withdraw his data from a study after his participation is otherwise completed, there are cases where the discontinuance of participation may take this form. This possibility becomes important when, for sufficient reasons, the investigator has found it necessary to withhold or distort information that is relevant to the participant's informed consent to participate (see Section 3-4). Thus, the following incident in which prior consent was not even obtained:

A psychologist was studying the expression of emotion in facial and body cues. During early research projects he filmed subjects without their knowledge, since it could be easily shown that knowledge of the fact that one was to be filmed affected the way in which the emotions were displayed. While he always obtained the patient's permission to use the films following the completion of the observation session, there was a pressure on him to persuade the subjects to agree to the use of the films because of his investment in the materials. Technological advances now permit this psychologist to record subjects' responses to various materials on videotape. Then it can be erased with no loss except for the time invested in the collecting of the data. This psychologist now specifies that the subject will be permitted to withhold consent for the use of the videotape, in which case it is erased before anyone but the cameraman sees it, and the subject is paid the fee for serving in any case. This psychologist remains concerned that it is necessary for the operator of the television camera to observe the subject's interaction with the experimenter unknown to the subject. However, he considers that the benefits from his work outweigh the ethical disadvantages of this amount of invasion of the subject's privacy.

Here the unwilling participant's right to withdraw his data effectively substitutes for his compromised right to refuse his consent to participate, and substantially mitigates the ethical difficulty.

In research employing deception in which the investigator subsequently explains the purposes and procedures of the study, the participant should be given the explicit opportunity to withdraw his data. In the more usual situation in which the participant's genuinely informed consent has been obtained prior to participation, spontaneously volunteered wishes to withdraw data should be respected, but the investigators are under no special obligation to raise the issue at the end of the research session.

Section 6. Fairness and Freedom from Exploitation in the Research Relationship

The relationship between the investigator and the research participant is one of mutual respect and involves considerations of fairness or equity. Each party to the relationship has expectations of the other, which in the ideal case will be accurate and congruent with one another. The agreement to take part in an experiment usually implies that the participant is willing to provide research data at some personal cost of time and effort and perhaps unpleasantness or risk in order to receive, in return, certain benefits. The expected benefits may be tangible rewards in the form of money or goods; they may be personal help such as counseling or therapy; they may be informational as, for example, a satisfactory explanation of the purposes of the experiment and its relationship to the current state of knowledge in some field. They also may be the satisfaction of feeling one has advanced science, helped solve a social problem, or done a favor for the researcher. Ethical problems arise when too much is asked of the participant given the anticipated benefits, when the investigator fails to keep his part of the bargain, and when he exploits the participant's personal circumstances in order to obtain cooperation.

The agreement between the investigator and the research participant can be evaluated from a dual perspective: (a) The agreement itself should be fair in the judgment of the participant. (b) The investigator should keep whatever promises he makes. Ideally there should be a reciprocal provision of benefits and good faith on the part of the participant, too, but we are concerned here only with the obligations of the investigator.

The researcher's obligations to the research participant are not easy to establish with clarity, for several reasons: (a) The expected and actual benefits to the participants are difficult to assess; (b) some potential participants—for example, mental patients, children, and the mentally defective—may not be able to understand the proposed agreement; (c) in other cases, the personal situation of the individual may influence what seems fair. A person feeling great need of some service such as psychotherapy would be willing to take greater risks and to sustain greater costs to obtain this help than would a person without such a felt need; (*d*) finally, some of the investigator's obligations exist only by reasons of the implications of the research setting. Such intangibles are, of course, particularly difficult to assess.

How explicit does the agreement between investigator and participant need to be? How can the investigator tread the thin line between offering adequate inducements to participate and exploitation (which amounts also to coercion to participate: See Principle 5)? When the possibility of exploitation is manifest, how may the responsible investigator nevertheless safeguard the interests of the participant? The complex ethical issues involved here are suggested in the following incidents.

Incidents

1. Subjects were recruited by promising to finance a party for each dormitory in which 90% volunteered to participate in a research project. While the task was not particularly stressful, the researchers worried that in order to reach the 90% quota, dormitory mates might have exerted undue social pressure on the few subjects who may have been too busy or squeamish to want to participate.

2. Admission to a low-cost cooperative rooming house for which many students have a great financial need, in a situation in which low-cost housing falls far short of the amount needed, is made conditional upon agreement to participate in research.

3. In studying the effect of overreward, the subjects were promised a very large sum of money for performing a task, and the quality of their work and liking for the task were measured after they completed it and were paid. When the purpose of the experiment was explained to them and they were asked to return the money, except for the $2.00 they were originally promised at the time of recruitment, all the subjects agreed to return the extra sum. The researcher felt that it was fair for him to ask the return of the extra money because it was a bonus that was mentioned to the subject only after he agreed to participate for the smaller sum that he was in fact allowed to keep.

4. All subjects in the course were promised information on the outcome of any experiments in which they volunteered to participate. But many of these experiments were not completed at the end of the semester and so could not be reported in class. Effort was seldom made to track down former subjects later, when the results were available.

Principle

The ethical investigator must be concerned with the fairness of whatever implicit or explicit agreements are made with the participants. He incurs the responsibility to assure that the participants' reasonable expectations are realized. In appraising the fairness of the agreement, the investigator must guard against exploiting the special needs and vulnerabilities of the potential participants to gain their cooperation. The guiding principle can be stated thus:

Principle 6.   Ethically acceptable research begins with the establishment of a clear and fair agreement between the investigator and the research participant that clarifies the responsibilities of each. The investigator has the obligation to honor all promises and commitments included in that agreement.

Discussion

Principle 6 states the three essential components of an appropriate agreement between investigator and participant, that the terms of the agreement be clear and explicit, that they be basically fair and not exploitative, and that the researcher honor the agreement. Prior to treating the problems associated with each of these portions of the agreement, around which this discussion will be organized, we first inquire about how explicit the agreement needs to be.

A.   *The Explicitness of the Agreement*

Actually, the question about explicitness is only another way of looking at the problems of informed consent and freedom from coercion to participate, already treated at length under Principles 3, 4, and 5, and no new considerations need to be introduced here. We have seen that there are sometimes reasons why an investigator may responsibly decide that it is warranted to compromise these ideals with respect to either the information provided or the opportunity for free consent. When the possible costs to the participant are more than trivial, we have seen that the investigator incurs serious ethical responsibility if the participant is deprived of these rights. By the same token, the more substantial the possible costs to the participant of his research involvement, the more essential it is that the research agreement be fully explicit. The kinds of procedures discussed under Principle 5 in connection with the administration of a "subject pool" for research on students in a university setting help assure a desirable degree of explicitness.

B.   *The Fairness of the Agreement*

The problems here are difficult and complex. If the participant is not to be exploited in the research situation, the agreement must be such that potential benefits stand in a reasonable relationship to the demands made of the participant. This means that the participant must be informed about the research conditions in enough detail to permit a competent judgment of the fairness of the agreement—again raising the issues of informed consent and freedom from coercion to participate. Since arranging the demands and benefits for individual participants might violate the most basic principles of experimental design, however, it will usually be necessary for the investigator to provide the same benefits to all participants. This adds to the complexities involved in developing an agreement that will be appropriate.

In judging the demands that are being made of the participant, consideration must be given to loss of time and freedom; to any boredom, physical or mental stress; or to loss of privacy to which the individual may be subjected. Benefits would include any financial payments; knowledge regarding himself, the problem being investigated or the research process; satisfaction from aiding the advancement of science or the solution of social problems; etc. But how are these factors to be weighed, one against the other, to insure that the arrangement is fair from the participant's point of view? There seem to be three points to make in attempting to answer this question: (*a*) If the investigator is alerted to the possible problem, he can make a judgment himself by imagining how he would react if he were a participant. In some cases the investigator may be able to arrive at a more realistic evaluation by participating in a preliminary study himself. (*b*) Recognizing that this answer is likely to be biased in favor of doing the research, the investigator can ask a few preliminary participants to serve in the study and, interviewing them, determine their perception of the fairness of the agreement. (*c*) It is also possible to turn to colleagues for help of two kinds: (*i*) suggestions for possible changes in procedure that might bring benefits and demands into better balance and (*ii*) advice on the question of whether the research is important enough so that the benefits it might yield over and above those accruing directly to the participant justify his proceeding despite excessive costs to the participant. Whenever the possibility of an equitable agreement is in doubt, ethical consultation is essential (Principle 1).

C. *Relationship between Participants' Needs and the Benefits Received*

In many research situations there is a congruent relationship between the needs of the participants and the type of benefits offered. But in other cases this is not so. To illustrate, consider the following incident:

> All students enrolled in introductory psychology and several other elementary courses were required to serve in three hours of experiments. It was argued that this was a valuable adjunct to the study of introductory psychology, but the specific experiments were not necessarily related to the subject matter of the course, and the requirement seemed more motivated to serve the convenience of researchers.

For students in introductory psychology, participation might well provide a benefit relevant to the need that got them into the course in the first place, the desire for psychological knowledge. For such students, it seems appropriate to reward them directly in these terms. Whether or not the knowledge provided is exactly coincident with the specific subject matter of the course, it should be a straightforward matter and a felt obligation for the researcher to work out an explanation of his investigation to contribute to the students' psychological education.

But how about the students in the "several other elementary courses"? If, as sometimes happens, these are not psychology students, the psychological knowledge provided by the researcher may be of little interest or value to the students. In such cases the investigator has an obligation to find some other benefit that would fulfill the students' actual needs. Failing that, he has the burden of assuring himself that the importance of the research to science or society is nevertheless great enough to justify doing it with participants drawn from such groups.

Still more difficult problems arise when participants enter the research agreement because of some very strong need. Again an incident will help to illustrate the problem:

> Financial rewards were used with the destitute or with impoverished prisoners, to have them participate in research involving drugs or high-stress conditions where it seemed likely that persons under ordinary circumstances would not participate even for a considerably larger financial inducement. One worries that the researcher was taking advantage of people whose need is so great . . . .

In such cases, the participant's need may be so desperate that, in effect, he cannot say No. Because the research agreement is thus coerced (in violation of Principle 5), the researcher may be guilty of exploitatively taking advantage of the participant's need. This is not to say that monetary rewards should never be given to poor persons in exchange for their participation in research. It would be grossly unfair to withhold from them the opportunity to receive such rewards just because they happen to need the money. It is rather to say that in cases of this sort, free consent *cannot* be assumed in spite of willing and explicit agreement, and it is incumbent upon the investigator to take special pains to assure that the participants' interests are protected and that the compromise of Principle 5 is warranted. The potentially high-cost procedures implied in the description of the incident would seem ill-advised under these circumstances.

In the type of case just considered, the participant at least knows what benefits to count upon, even though his extreme need may have coerced the choice to participate. The problem becomes more difficult when the researcher cannot specify the benefits hoped for with any assurance, as in the case when research participation is made a condition of receiving therapeutic help. The therapeutic outcomes may be quite uncertain, so that the participant may be willing to strike a dubious bargain because of his wishful thinking. Again, the special precautions called for when free consent cannot be assumed are in order. The investigator should guard against playing upon the wishful thinking of the participant in need.

In the following incident, the investigator may have aroused expectations that seem likely to go unfulfilled:

> Members of a severely deprived minority group were asked to participate in research on the grounds that the results of the research could be essential for the well-being of their group.

Inducing participation in anticipation of benefits to the participants' major reference groups is in violation of Principle 6 unless the investigator is in a confident position to deliver on his promises.

Finally, special problems arise when the researcher artificially creates needs (usually in the process of recruiting) that may then enter into the participants' perception of the agreement arrived at with the investigator. Consider this incident:

> When patients were recruited for an experiment, it was implied to them that if they did not cooperate it would be a sign of immaturity and might adversely affect staff evaluation of the patient.

Such tactics not only involve an inappropriately coercive threat, but they imply, riskily, that cooperation in the experiment will be rewarded by perception of the patient by investigator and staff as more mature—not something that can confidently be promised to psychiatric patients. The researcher has allowed the agreement with the participants to include elements that are almost certain to leave the patient with unrealistic expectations. This procedure seems also to take advantage exploitatively of the patients' vulnerability and even to augment it.

D.   *Fulfilling the Agreement with the Participant*

A part of what is involved here has already been covered in the previous section, where we saw that taking advantage of a person's strong needs to induce him to participate without his being adequately free to refuse may create expectations in the participant that the researcher cannot fulfill. When he encourages the participant in developing such expectations, implicit or explicit, intentional or not, the researcher incurs an obligation to satisfy them.

Moreover, it should be clear that more than just promises directly related to the research procedures are involved. Research takes place in a social context which always has its implications. For example, a part of what participants rightfully expect is respectful treatment. Because the researcher is paying the participants or exacting required research participation from them, there is always the possibility that this will unconsciously be accepted by both parties as the entire definition of the relationship. The intent of Principle 6 is broader than that. Accordingly, the behavior of the experimenter described in the following incident is ethically unacceptable:

> The researcher was the type of person who seldom showed up anywhere on time and during the experiment almost invariably showed up about 15 minutes late, keeping the subject waiting. He said that he was paying the subject for an hour and the experiment took only a half hour, so even with his lateness the subject was getting a good deal. But it seemed to me that the lateness was insulting to the subject and that he was losing a quarter-hour's time just because the experimenter lacked self-discipline.

In general the agreement to participate typically includes the participant's expectation that the researcher will treat *him* with courtesy, consideration, and respect, and the investigator has an obligation to behave appropriately.

E. *Classes of Participants Whose Own Consent Must Be Supplemented by That of Another*

The rationale of the research agreement cannot apply without modification when young children, disturbed patients, or the mentally retarded are involved. As noted in the discussion of the corresponding point under obtaining informed consent to participate (Principle 3), there are both legal and ethical requirements to come to an explicit agreement with a responsible person who can base his decision on an appraisal of the prospective participant's best interests. Having done this, the investigator continues to have an obligation to treat the participant himself with respect. Such treatment requires as explicit and understandable an agreement as the participant can grasp, and the honoring of all promises.

Section 7. Protection from Physical and Mental Stress

In most psychological research, the participants are exposed neither to appreciable physical suffering or danger nor to appreciable mental stress. The relatively rare studies involving physical stress or danger are typically undertaken to clarify important topics such as motivation or the nature of pain and its relief. The investigator may be studying the stressful state itself (e.g., the effects of drugs on pain suppression), or he may use deprivation, electric shock, or intense noise to manipulate motivational or incentive conditions.

Mental stress also is absent from most psychological research, but in some studies it may arise as an essential aspect, in others, incidentally, and in still others, accidentally. It may be the essential independent variable, as when the researcher exposes participants to varying levels of failure in order to study the effects of loss of self-esteem on ways of coping or to temptations to lie or cheat in order to study moral functioning and development. In other studies, the mental stress involves a less essential aspect of the research, as when different levels of anxiety are induced in order to study the effects of drive level on stimulus generalization. In still other cases, the mental stress involves a less essential aspect of the research, as when different levels of anxiety are induced in order to study the effects of drive level on stimulus generalization. In still other cases, the mental stress arises accidentally, as when some participants are embarrassed by certain questionnaire items in ways difficult to anticipate or when the participant unexpectedly develops feelings of having done poorly on a learning task.

Responsible investigators obviously would not expose research participants to actual or potential physical or mental harm if there were not a very serious reason for doing so. Although some psychologists feel that such research should be entirely prohibited, the dominant view in the field is probably that when such studies are important they should be continued. Under what circumstances is research involving physical or mental stress or danger permissible?

Studies that raise this question are relatively rare partly because investigators are ingenious enough to find alternate ways of studying the research problem at issue. For example, much research on deprivation employs non-human animals, or uses deprivations or stresses that are relatively trivial in type and amount, or studies persons who are undergoing differential amounts of deprivation or mental stress for reasons independent of the research and beyond the investigator's control.

Where such alternatives cannot be found, might the importance of the research counterbalance the appreciable costs to the participant? When the investigator decides that research involving physical or mental stress is warranted, what measures should be taken to protect the welfare of the participants?

The range of kinds of mental or physical stress that may present ethical issues for decision is very large and is suggested by the following incidents, grouped according to whether physical or mental stress is involved.

Incidents

Physical Stress, Danger, and Drugs

1. I directed a series of studies concerning the effects of heat, noise, altitude, and vibration on human performance in physiology. All of these studies involved considerable discomfort for the subjects. Physical danger was also present, since there was always the possibility that one of the control systems might fail and expose the subject to unacceptably high levels of stress (e.g., an electronic malfunction in the vibration control system could result in a broken back); there was also the possibility that an undiscovered medical defect (e.g., a fused spinal vertebrae) could render a subject unable to tolerate stresses that would be acceptable for normal subjects.

We adopted the following objectives to lessen danger to the subjects: (*a*) to minimize the probability of damaging one of the subjects; (*b*) to ensure that the subjects fully understood the nature and extent of the risks they were taking; (*c*) to ensure that participation in the experiments was completely voluntary.

These objectives were achieved as follows: (*a*) One week of failure-free operation of the laboratory facilities was required prior to the start of any experiment; (*b*) a full complement of safety monitoring equipment (electronic and mechanical); (*c*) a full-time medical monitor during all experimental testing; (*d*) complete review of all experimental procedures and stress levels by medical personnel who were not involved in the research program; (*e*) prior to each experiment the principal investigator (myself) exposed himself to higher levels of stress than those to be used in the experiment; (*f*) complete medical examination of all subjects before testing, and any subject who deviated from normal was rejected; (*g*) prior to testing, each subject was given a detailed description of the test plan which he was required to read before deciding whether to serve as a subject; (*h*) each subject observed a complete test run (either on one of the experimenters or on another subject) before deciding to serve; (*i*) a "scare lecture" was given to each subject describing in detail the possible medical consequences of a system failure (broken back, broken ear drums, heat prostration, permanent hearing loss, etc.); (*j*) after the subject had studied the test plan, observed a test run, and received the "scare lecture," he was required to sign a voluntary consent form; (*k*) a complete medical record was maintained throughout all testing (heart rate, body temperature, respiratory rate), and a copy was made available to the subject. In six years of testing, there were no system failures when a subject was being tested (there were a number when experimenters were being tested). In one instance a potential subject with fused vertebrae managed to pass the medical examination; however, the "scare lecture" brought this out, and the subject was rejected.

2.   A graduate student proposed studying the immediate effects of a standard dosage of LSD-25 upon the behavior and physiological status of adult male subjects. The proposal raised the following ethical issues: immediate safety of his subjects, potential consequences of postexperimental residuals (interference with driving skills, mood swings, disorientation, etc.), possible long-range effects (further drug experimentation on own, histological changes in somatic and sex cells, emotional or adjustment disruptions, etc.).

The solutions worked out were as follows: (*a*) recruitment of subjects over the age of 21 from professional school populations (medical school, dental school) who would be best informed and able to make an informed and reasoned decision to volunteer for the study when told of the drug and the purpose of the investigation; (*b*) explicit payment of the subjects for their participation; (*c*) experimental sessions carried out with close medical collaboration in a hospital setting, even though this selection of research context undoubtedly introduced some special sets in the research subjects; (*d*) continuous monitoring of the physiological status of the subjects and regular interviews, observational samplings from the research booth as well as the use of standard tests for gathering dependent variable data; (*e*) administration of best known antidote at the end of the seven-hour session with provision for (*i*) someone to take the subject home who would also be able to stay with him the remainder of the night (roommate, spouse), and (*ii*) admission to the hospital overnight with appropriate nursing surveillance; (*f*) contact with subject the following day for further interviewing and retesting; (*g*) follow-up on a long-range basis after graduating from professional school and beginning career involving questionnaires on health, drug usage, attitudes toward drugs, and personal and professional changes as well as readministration of the standard tests.

Mental Stress

1.   The experiment involved showing pictures of distorted faces bearing gunshot wounds, drowning victims, etc., to college students. Before the study was conducted, the question arose as to whether some individuals would experience very strong emotional reactions to such pictures, perhaps even some lasting disturbance. As a result, we had these pictures shown to the staff at the counseling center, several graduate students in psychology and a small sampling of undergraduate students. Most of these people found the pictures to be aversive

but did not experience unusually strong reactions. During the main experiment, which involved galvanic skin response recording, subjects were given the option of stopping the experiment if they found it to be too unpleasant, but none of the subjects took advantage of this opportunity.

2. A social psychologist attached a psycho-galvanometer to subjects (male college students). The participants were told that the needle would be deflected if they were aroused, and that if the needle deflected when they viewed photographs of nude males, it would indicate latent homosexuality. Then false feedback was given so that the subjects were led to believe incorrectly that they were latent homosexuals. After the experiment, the ruse was explained.

Principle

The researcher may find himself in conflict between the obligation to carry out research which he feels might yield important human benefits and the obligation to avoid treating participants in that research in ways that are likely to expose them to appreciable levels of physical or mental stress. In resolving these conflicting obligations, the researcher must weigh the amount and probability of the stress which he is likely to produce and the number of participants who might experience it against the possible benefits that the research might yield. Research that involves physical or mental stress or risk of harm may be conducted only for highly important purposes and only after a thorough search for alternatives to minimize danger or discomfort. A decision that such a study is ethically warranted requires that safeguards to protect the participant be commensurate with the stress or risk that is involved. Such a decision may be reached responsibly only after full technical and ethical consultation. Principle 7 summarizes the investigator's responsibilities. It implies that the principles relating to informed consent to participate (Principle 3), to fairness and freedom from exploitation in the research relationship (Principle 6), and to removal of stressful consequences following completion of the research (Principle 9) must be scrupulously observed—with compromise in these principles not to be tolerated insofar as the stress or risk is serious.

Principle 7. The ethical investigator protects participants from physical and mental discomfort, harm and danger. If the risk of such consequences exists, the investigator is required to inform the participant of that fact, secure consent before proceeding, and take all possible measures to minimize distress. A research procedure may not be used if it is likely to cause serious and lasting harm to participants.

Discussion

Because the specific contexts of ethical decision differ for physical stress and danger, on the one hand, and mental stress on the other, the two situations will be discussed separately.

Physical Stress, Danger, and Drugs

A.   *Types of Research That Involve Physical Discomforts and Dangers*

In some types of psychological research the occurrence of appreciable physical discomfort is certain. Studying various aspects of pain (including its physiological basis, determinants of its intensity, or ways of ameliorating it), for example, is likely to involve exposing participants to pain. In other research, physical discomfort is centrally—if less essentially—involved as a way of manipulating the participant's motivation. For example, the participant is deprived of food or water for appreciable periods, or a negative reinforcer such as electric shock or loud noise is used to eliminate erroneous responses. Other studies expose the participants to very unpleasant tastes, extreme temperature, or other special states which are likely to produce an appreciable amount of discomfort. Obtaining certain kinds of physiological indices also entails some degree of physical discomfort. For example, obtaining blood samples, which might be quite tolerable to most participants, may be highly disturbing to a few.

One type of research that deserves special mention is the administration of drugs that have a high likelihood of causing appreciable adverse direct or side effects and so raise issues comparable to the other stressful treatments just mentioned. In addition, drugs involve additional dangers such as the possibility of causing addiction and violating legal regulations, and special problems arise in obtaining informed consent while yet avoiding spurious suggestion effects by giving information about the drug.

There are a variety of other conditions where serious danger or discomfort is much less likely to occur, but remains a worrisome possibility because of equipment failures, the involvement of particularly susceptible participants, or other accidents hard to anticipate. Included here would be such procedures as cardiac conditioning, inducement of high levels of fatigue, or the use of recording techniques that may produce anxiety because they are not fully understood by the participant. The researcher must be sufficiently familiar with his area of work to appreciate such unlikely but serious possibilities, take measures to lessen their likelihood, and anticipate what is to be done if they should occur. These issues are considered more fully in subsequent sections. The following incidents illustrate problems just mentioned:

We conducted a subliminal conditioning experiment using shock as the UCS. The experiment was designed so that the participant could set his own level of shock. A standard stimulator was used. When the shock was turned to zero and the first stimulation was given, the participant yelled to turn the shock down. On further checking, we discovered 110 volts coming from the stimulator (with very low current). The moral is that the experimenter must check the experimental apparatus in the experimental situation — not just separately. Also, he should check it on himself, not on the participant or graduate assistant. In this case, fortunately the participant was not seriously burned but his good will and cooperation were lost and very bad public relations within the department resulted.

A PhD candidate prepared a thesis proposal for an experiment involving reactions to pain stimuli. Pain was to be evoked by a technique of tightening a band about the participant's head to establish the limiting intensity of pain he was willing to endure. The technique was recommended because of its reliability as established by previous research. Participants were to be volunteers, well paid and thoroughly advised in advance of the nature of the pain and discomfort they would experience if they agreed to serve.

The department ethics committee turned down this proposed research as being unjustifiably stressful. The student's thesis advisor and thesis commiteee members were absolutely outraged, contending that it was ridiculous to object to a procedure which caused no permanent injury and merely involved momentary pain, the limits of which were to be determined by the participant.

B.   *Alternative Procedures to Avoid Physical Stress*

To the extent that research involves an appreciable possibility of physical discomfort or danger, the investigator is obligated to search for substitute techniques that might avoid such experiences. One possibility is the use of nonhuman animals instead of human, as is frequently done in studies of deprivation and aversive reinforcement. One is obliged to treat lower animals as well as people humanely, but current ethical standards usually permit a higher level of physical risk to nonhuman animals in important research.

Some studies to ascertain the effectiveness of a new treatment involve using a control group that is deprived of a possible benefit, for example, a "placebo" group, to test the benefits of a new drug. The investigator contemplating such a design might consider lessening the deprivation of the control group by giving them a treatment of known effectiveness rather than no treatment.

Some research on stress may be possible by studying persons undergoing stressful conditions as part of their inevitable life experiences, so that the investigator need not inflict physical discomfort. An investigator interested in ascertaining ways of ameliorating pain through the use of hypnosis, for example, might avoid the use of pain-inflicting procedures by selecting participants who are already experiencing unavoidable pain because of therapeutic procedures, illness, or the like. However, ethical problems do arise when the investigator, for research purposes, allows such stress-producing situations to continue by withholding possible alleviating treatments.

When some level of physical discomfort is judged to be necessary and tolerable in order to study a sufficiently significant problem, the researcher should be quite careful to keep the discomfort at a minimum. Even when it is judged permissible to use electric shock, aversive noise levels, and the like, the levels should be set sufficiently low, on the basis of pretests and personal participation, so that they would not be experienced as intolerable even by the more sensitive participants among those who pass a careful screening procedure. The following incident points up the problems of inadequate background knowledge and insufficient screening studies with animals by the experimenter:

Another investigator proceeded to place human participants, some of whom were hospitalized psychiatric cases and others who were volunteer college students, in high-energy electromagnetic fields as part of an overall program to study the effects of magnetic fields on performance. The investigator admitted to knowing little, if anything, about marginally destructive energy levels in this situation. Later, in a study with spider monkeys, it was found that the energy level used previously with humans was destructive of cortical tissue. The volunteers were naive with respect to possible damage that might result from their participating in the experiment. To my knowledge, the only resolution of the ethical dilemma posed by the new data was that the investigator intends to "be more careful" when working with humans again.

C. Safety Precautions to Minimize Possible Dangers to the Participants

It is the researcher's obligation to be fully informed of the possible dangers involved in any of the procedures used. Some procedures involve sufficiently clear and present dangers so that any reasonable investigator will perceive the need for a number of precautions. For example, even when special circumstances may justify the administration of electric shocks to adequately informed and freely consenting participants, the investigator obviously owes it to the participant to take a variety of precautions. For one thing, the investigators and any assistants should be thoroughly trained in the physical and physiological factors involved in electric shocks and with the particular apparatus used. They must assure that the equipment is in a state which eliminates any appreciable likelihood that dangerous shock levels can be administered either through mechanical failure or misuse. Moreover, he must ascertain that the participants do not suffer from any special medical conditions that would make the levels of shocks to be used in any way dangerous to them. Also, emergencies that might arise must be considered, and appropriate preparations must be made to deal with them.

In the case of other treatments with potential dangers comparable to that of administering electric shocks, the research should take similarly appropriate safety precautions including training, selection and pretesting of the equipment, screening participants, and emergency plans to deal with accidents. There is probably greater likelihood that appropriate safety procedures will be neglected when the researcher employs techniques that are less obviously dangerous. Even with seemingly innocuous procedures, it is the investigator's responsibility to anticipate accidents, and to take appropriate safety precautions. The following incident illustrates appropriate procedures in this kind of study:

A graduate student was interested in whether the Wechsler Adult Intelligence Scale Digit Span subtest performance is influenced by anxiety level, with the level of anxiety manipulated by varying the level of electric shock. The potential ethical problems associated with the use of noxious stimulation were handled as follows: (a) The student surveyed the literature to determine levels of shock administered to human subjects by other investigators; (b) he evaluated the possibility that an electrical malfunction in his equipment could deliver a shock of greater intensity than intended; (c) he administered the various levels of shock to himself and several fellow graduate students (which, incidentally, led to using a maximum shock level lower than originally intended); and (d) subjects were told that the study was an investigation of the effects of distracting stimulation on intellectual performance and that for some subjects the distracting stimulation would be an electric shock. No subject had to participate in the experiment.

D. *Screening Out Susceptible Participants in Research Involving Physical Discomfort or Danger*

Where special circumstances lead to the judgment that it is permissible to expose participants to physical discomfort or danger, it is usually necessary to eliminate certain classes of people from the pool of participants. For example, studies of pain that might be judged permissible with fully informed and freely volunteering college students would be judged unsuitable for children because they might be less familiar with such experiences and terrified by them or because their fundamental trust might be violated. Again, it would be inappropriate to use patients or other clients who depend for services upon the institution sponsoring the research (e.g., the mentally ill, the very old, or hospitalized patients) because they might not adequately appreciate that participation is voluntary and strictly for research or grasp the level of discomfort likely to be experienced.

Even with the normal adult population, the researcher must be aware of the wide range of individual differences in susceptibility to the discomforts and dangers involved in various physical stresses. Unrecognized physical defects or allergies, for example, might make a seemingly healthy individual particularly susceptible to an experimental drug or particularly sensitive to some type of discomfort-causing stimulus. The investigator, therefore, is obliged to be familiar with such conditions that heighten susceptibility and to recognize and screen out of the research those people who have such conditions. For example, a study of the effects of alcohol that varied the dose well within limits deemed appropriate for most persons might be completely unacceptable for people with tendencies toward alcoholism. Where new drugs or possibly harmful procedures are involved, they should be checked first with animals. The researcher should also be aware that in some lines of research (e.g., those involving drugs, biofeedback to alter physiological states, or hypnosis) certain persons need to be protected against themselves. That is, free and informed consent is not enough; the researcher should be aware that the very enthusiasm of some persons to take part in such research may be symptomatic of the need to screen these people out of the study.

The two incidents that follow highlight the issues described in this section:

The use of beverage alcohol in research with both alcoholics and nonalcoholics raises several ethical issues: (*a*) Alcoholics in particular may be led to drink excessively as a function of participating in studies involving drinking; (*b*) giving alcohol to alcoholics may violate established guidelines for the treatment of alcoholism which involves encouraging total abstinence on the part of the alcoholic; (*c*) alcohol may be particularly harmful for people with certain medical problems such as ulcers or liver damage; (*d*) automobile and industrial accidents may follow even the minimal ingestion of alcohol.

In our experiments with alcohol, we restricted our sample of alcoholic subjects to hospitalized patients upon whom we were able to exert an appropriate degree of control with which to protect both them and the community from harm. All subjects were asked if there were medical contraindications to their drinking in a study, and, in addition, the patients were screened medically.

The study concerned the effects of aversive stimulation (white noise of high intensity) on various reaction time measures of hospitalized male psychiatric patients, mostly schizophrenics. Previous research in this area reported using noise levels of 116 decibels. These studies had been done by reputable researchers. Although also interested in maximizing the effects of this negative input, I seriously questioned the use of 116 decibels, since various sources now claim that serious and permanent ear damage can occur with noise levels at or close to 116 decibels.

I finally settled on a noise level of 90 decibels, purely subjectively. That is, I graded the noise level (which was fed in over a pair of earphones) by listening to it myself and settling on the intensity which was immensely uncomfortable, but still bearable for short periods, *for me*. In the absence of absolute parameters and of complete agreement in this area as to what the limits of such aversive stimulation ought to be, there was some comfort to me in knowing that I would not subject anyone else to procedures which I would not tolerate, condone, or accept without undue duress for myself.

I realize that the above need not have been a very realistic guarantee, because individuals vary in their tolerance levels or thresholds. I did not attempt to obtain any such threshold on the subjects. Thus, it is possible that what was barely acceptable to me, might have been quite beyond that for some more sensitive patient. This I see as a criticism of many studies, not only from an "ethical" but also, of course, from a scientific point of view.

E.   *Dangerous Research Treatments Benefitting the Participant*

The investigator must be especially careful not to expose certain classes of people, such as children and patients, to considerable physical discomfort or danger solely for research purposes. However, exposing persons to stressful conditions solely for research purposes should be distinguished from doing research in situations where therapeutic or diagnostic procedures are used for the possible benefit of the participants themselves. Here the major consideration is the justifiability of procedures that involve additional physical discomfort or pain only for research purposes. Although the diagnostician or therapist should be cautious in the use of dangerous procedures, even for the patient's benefit, it may be reasonable to tolerate a higher likelihood of adverse effects when the treatment is being employed for the possible benefit of the participant than when it is being employed strictly for research purposes. The following incident illustrates the difficult questions that such research–therapeutic procedures might raise:

We used electric shock to eliminate undesirable self-destructive behavior in a 10-year-old female child with a normal IQ. After trying *satiation* and *incompatible response* procedures with some, but not with complete success, I used a cattle prod, operated by the child's father. The ethical issue was: Should I have used electric shock, and should parents have been directly involved? My solution was to try other procedures first. Meanwhile, the father had read about *aversive therapy* and suggested it; after an extensive interview, during which the electric shocks were given to the father so that he could better appreciate their effects, I was convinced he could follow instructions and administer shock in a systematic manner.

F.   *Necessity for Continued Assurance of Freedom to End Participation at Any Point*

The importance of assuring that the participant takes part in research only by his or her free and informed consent is discussed at a number of places in this document (Sections 3-4 and 5). The point needs particular emphasis with studies that involve any appreciable physical discomfort or danger. The researcher should be sensitive to subtle pressures that limit the participant's effective freedom to decline taking part in the study. For example, in studies involving pain, the researcher should particularly avoid recruitment procedures such as talking the person into participation on the basis of the importance of the work to science or society. Also, the investigator must be sensitive to the possibility that men may feel participation to be a test of their masculinity and so either anticipate and experience the pain with great trepidation or decline to participate with serious loss of self-esteem. In these situations, the researcher should try to relieve the person of any negative feelings or self-doubts about refusal to participate. Although it might be difficult for the researcher to "load the dice" against himself in the quest for suitable participants, he is obliged to be sensitive to these issues.

Furthermore, the investigator should be especially careful in situations involving physical stress to assure that the person remains aware that participation can be terminated at any point. Particularly, there should be no pressure on the individual to continue if reluctance to go on with the study is indicated. But more than this, the researcher should be constantly vigilant for any signs of incipient reluctance by the participant and should make it clear during the procedure that termination is possible at any time. The following incident illustrates some of the issues discussed:

A researcher was conducting research on pain at a medical school by using a headband with numerous screws that could be tightened by hand to press against the subject's head. According to the experimenter's published report, subjects were solicited mainly from medical students at the university. On the basis of interviews conducted after the experiment, the experimenter reported that the subjects participated for the following reasons: (a) to contribute to science; (b) because they thought it was a requirement for a course they were enrolled in; (c) because they feared the effect refusal to participate might have on their grades; (d) because they wished not to alienate the experimenter, who was also their teacher and had considerable power over them and their fate in medical school. In one experiment reported, the subjects were told to endure the pain inflicted by the head apparatus as long as they possibly could. The instructions stressed the importance of enduring the pain just as long as it was possible to do so. After one of the subjects reported that he could endure the pain no longer, the experimenter mentioned to him that others had endured it much longer and, in various ways, by threatening the subject's masculinity and self-image, he induced the subject to continue to wear the headband for a substantially longer period of time.

G. Problems Regarding Informed Consent in Research Involving Administration of Drugs and Other Treatments Whose Effects Might Be Obscured by Suggestions

In studies on drug effects with human participants, the investigator must control for spurious effects resulting from the participant's suggestibility. That is, if fully informed about the nature of the drug and its possible direct or side effects, the participant might experience these effects because of having been told that they might occur rather than because of the chemical action of the drugs. The investigator is thus caught in a conflict of values: Either the research is carried out without obtaining the participant's fully informed consent, or it is carried out with the danger that the fully informed participant might show effects due to suggestion, or one must forego the research that might have led to important human benefits.

The responsible investigator must attempt to resolve such a conflict in a way that takes account of the various elements in this dilemma. It may be possible, for example, to withhold some of the specific details about possible effects of the drug, provided that it is made clear to the participant that drugs are indeed being administered and that they might produce discomforts or dangers of specific magnitude (even if the specific nature of these possible effects is not made explicit). Then the researcher should, at any point where it seems required for the well-being of the participants (and certainly at the end of the study), fully inform the participants of the specific symptoms that might be experienced in connection with the drug.

The two incidents that follow provide examples of the ethical problems discussed in this section:

In a research project involving comparisons of effects of LSD, Ritalin, and placebo it was judged desirable not to inform subjects of the common name of the drugs involved because of the expectations that the patient would have, particularly about LSD. A signed consent form was obtained for each patient in which he was informed that he would receive a drug or saline, but only the chemical names of the drugs were given along with a statement of the possible helpful and harmful effects of the drugs. It was known that most patients would not recognize the chemical name of LSD, and it is possible that some subjects would have refused to participate in the research project had they known that they might be administered LSD. The issue was never resolved. The patients were just asked to sign the informed consent form with only the technical name of the drug appearing thereon. Legally, the research was covered, but ethically, I am not so sure.

In early tests of psychoactive medication not only double-blind procedures but also experimental naivete were needed to clarify drugs versus placebo or suggestion effects. To tell the patients exactly what we were administering to them would have made the study absolutely meaningless—in fact, some of us felt that telling them that research was being done biased the results. We coped with these problems by increasing our samples to include all kinds of experimental groups—thus making experimenter's instruction a source of variation. Our findings convinced us that deception was necessary and, therefore, we employed certain forms which were legal waivers but which were explained in "bureaucratese"—this made it possible to study all but paranoid subjects.

This is a real dilemma because complete honesty about drug tests means that the active medication must overcome a very strong placebo effect prior to being classified as active—thus, honesty to the experimental participant about the placebo deprives us of the opportunity to distinguish the psychological from the physiological (pharmacological) effect of a drug-taking regimen.

H.   *Legal Aspects of Research Involving Administration of Drugs*

Administration of drugs that involve the possibility of discomfort or danger to the recipient raises all the problems considered above inherent in other physically stressful treatments. But there are also legal problems peculiar to drug research. The use of certain drugs is proscribed by law even for research purposes. And where the administration of certain dangerous drugs is legal in research contexts, there are often legal restrictions or obligations imposed on the researcher that raise special dangers of criminal penalties to the institutions, or the participant. Hence, the researcher planning to administer drugs as part of a research project should make certain that he has observed the appropriate legal safeguards. At a minimum, it is important to ascertain that the drug has been obtained legally, used under conditions specified by federal and state laws, and has been appropriately tested. As is true for all drug studies with human beings, the researcher should be familiar with the known effects of the drug and conduct the research with whatever medical collaboration is prescribed by the law.

Finally, researchers studying illegal drug use should be especially mindful that the requirements of anonymity and confidentiality apply in their studies with a special force. For there might well be situations in which information obtained from the participant about his use of illegal drugs is requested by law enforcement agencies. The drug researcher should be particularly sensitive to this possibility and should make clear to the participant, when obtaining consent to participate, the extent to which the participant's anonymity and the confidentiality of the data will be protected in the face of legal demands. (See Principle 10 on the protection of confidentiality.) The following incident illustrates the neglect of several of the precautions noted above:

> Studies have been carried out on the effects of drugs (marijuana in particular) on personality traits, perception, ESP ability, etc. The studies were run "illegally" since the procurement of the drug was through an illegal source and the projects did not have government approval. The subjects were all users of the drugs and volunteers.

> The problem of ethics involved here as I see it is: The studies were worth doing since we were dealing with an area where facts, not guesswork, are needed. Although not directly involved, I had to give a "moral blessing" to get the studies going. After a great deal of thought I told the experimenters to go ahead if they wished, keeping in mind the laws on possession of marijuana.

Mental Stress

A. *Types of Mental Stress Produced in Psychological Research*

As in any situation involving human relations, insulting and thoughtless behavior on the part of the researcher can cause distress in the participants. The present discussion deals not with such negligence or crudeness on the part of researchers—which is clearly reprehensible—but rather with situations in which the research procedures cause mental distress to the participants, either as an essential part of the investigation, as an incidental part, or as an accidental side effect.

In some psychological studies, the essential independent variable involves inducing a certain amount of psychological stress. For example, fear and anxiety are manipulated to study the effects of conflict and frustration; or self-esteem is varied by failure experience or other manipulations. In some studies, the individual's shame or guilt is aroused, at least potentially, by exposing him to opportunities and temptations to lie, cheat, steal, or by pressure to inflict suffering on other people. In still other studies, the variable under investigation require exposing the individual to unpleasant materials, such as presenting him with words or pictures that arouse sexual anxiety or guilt, or with violent material or scenes of extreme human suffering. Or the unpleasantness might take the form of asking him to reveal personal data that he finds embarrassing or to perform disturbing tasks such as making ratings on his parents. In still other studies the mental stress is caused inadvertently, as when the experience proves more disturbing or tedious than the researcher anticipated. The following three incidents are illustrative:

An experimenter chided his subjects for slowness while they were performing an assigned task in order to elevate their blood pressure and other autonomic indicants. As a consequence, the subjects were angered and resented the treatment even after being informed when the experiment was completed.

In research using behavior modification techniques, live but harmless snakes were used to produce avoidance reactions and physiological responses. Subjects were given no prior warning, in order to assess responses to unexpected stimuli.

The design of a study of human reactions to psychological stress involved having subjects witness a film depicting mutilation of the human body. The volunteer subjects were told only that their reactions to the film were the objects of the study. They were not told that the film was stressful or possibly harmful. The basic assumption of the study was that the film would produce human stress reactions comparable in quality, though not necessarily in intensity, to naturally occurring stress reactions of clinical significance. The subjects were given a poststress interview during which catharsis was encouraged and, if they seemed sufficiently disturbed, were offered psychotherapy. In the judgment of the experimenter, none of the subjects was sufficiently disturbed by the film to warrant psychotherapy.

It is the investigator's obligation to anticipate the likelihood that the study might impose an appreciable amount of mental stress on the participant, and if this seems likely the research should be stopped unless there is compelling reason to continue. That is, it must be ascertained that the importance of the research justifies the level of stress likely to be involved, and, where possible, the informed participant as well as the investigator must agree that such is the case. Also, the researcher is obliged to seek less stressful ways of conducting the research and to take steps to minimize the level and duration of mental stress experienced.

B. *Monitoring for Unintended Mental Stress*

Any reasonable investigator will be aware that studies such as the ones discussed above will likely result in appreciable mental stress for the participants. But it is also necessary to recognize that a variety of other research procedures might accidentally result in certain kinds of mental stress. Participants sometimes prove to be more vulnerable than the investigator had anticipated; for example, they may conclude on the basis of their performance on a memory task that they did very poorly and thus feel inadequate. In other studies, participants may be disturbed at being asked certain questions that the researcher assumed were quite innocuous; for example, the investigator might fail to anticipate that asking some children from fatherless homes to state the name of father and mother might prove a stressful and embarrassing task.

C. Substitute Procedures to Avoid Causing Mental Stress

Experienced investigators who work on the important problems that involve mental stress have demonstrated that these problems can sometimes be studied using naturally occurring conditions. For example, rather than inducing anxiety, it is sometimes possible to study individuals in unavoidable anxiety-producing natural circumstances. Illustrative of such opportunities are students before and after an important examination and persons who are awaiting their turn in the dentist's chair. Ethical issues arise when the use of such occasions for research implicates the investigator in events with which one ought not to allow oneself to be associated (the Nazi death camp is an extreme case), or intrudes unacceptably upon human privacy or dignity (some research on dying patients might be so regarded).

Ohter researchers have been able to gain insight into such variables by using role-played simulated experiments in which the participants report how they would behave in a certain situation (e.g., whether or not they would have told a lie under one or another type of inducement).

In all of these substitute procedures, however, there are serious questions about the validity of the results. Whether results obtained using such substitute procedures are adequate, needs to be tested through systematic empirical studies. Because of the clear need for a better understanding of such important but highly sensitive phenomena, the investigator must weigh the costs of inadequate or misleading results against the moral costs of causing psychological stress to research participants.

D. The Necessity of Minimizing the Level and Duration of Mental Stress

The investigator, convinced of the importance of the problem being studied, is naturally inclined to make sure that the independent variable is manipulated sufficiently to permit its effects to be discernible. Hence, when the effects of variables such as anxiety or loss of self-esteem are being studied, there is some inclination to induce extreme levels of these variables for methodological purposes. This conflicts with the obligation to minimize the amount of such mental stress to which the participants are exposed. One resolution of this conflict is to lower the level of stress induction to the minimum that promises to be effective—even though this risks null results. Another, to be explored whenever possible, is to manipulate the variable in the favorable direction, lowering rather than raising anxiety and increasing rather than decreasing self-esteem.

E. *Special Problems of Obtaining Informed Consent to Participate in Research Involving Mental Stress*

As indicated in Principle 3, the researcher is obligated to employ as participants only those who have freely consented to serve when fully knowledgeable about all aspects of the research experience that might reasonably be expected to influence their decision to participate. If the research may involve mental stress, obviously one of the important things to inform them about is the possibility of this type of discomfort. This often raises a dilemma, because the stress-producing experience cannot be revealed in advance. For example, typically the participant must experience failure under circumstances whose believability would be considerably lessened if the investigator warned of the possibility of such a failure experience; or the research requirements might be that the participant be given an opportunity to cheat or steal, supposedly without the researcher's knowledge, so that an advance warning of such moral temptations would make the situation less meaningful. Consider, for example, the following incident:

> In order to obtain an estimate of how certain ongoing cognitive processes were affected by startling information and unfinished business irrelevant to the immediate task at hand, it became necessary to deceive the subject. A radio was playing in the laboratory waiting room, occasionally giving news reports. One of these was especially prepared, giving dramatic news of a sharp escalation of the Vietnam war (the study was done in 1964-65 in the early stages of American involvement). Mention of increased draft calls was included (many of the details in this simulated broadcast ultimately became realities in 1967-68). The subjects were obviously affected by the broadcast, but when ushered into their cubicles for the next stage of the experiment, did not refuse to participate. At the end of an hour of experimental procedures, subjects were questioned in detail about their reaction and the nature of the deception was carefully explained. Subjects were told why it was necessary to do this in order to insure that our research had a realistic relationship to the mental health issues of everyday life.

The decision on the part of the investigator to go ahead with a study in which the participants are exposed without prior warning to appreciable levels of mental stress raises serious ethical concerns. When the researcher concludes that it is indeed obligatory to proceed without a warning to the participant, people more concerned for the participants' well-being than with the progress of the research should be consulted in order to check out one's own judgment in the matter. Also, each person should be carefully interviewed after participation to make sure that the effect of the stress is minimized as much as possible (see Principle 9).

F.   Special Problems of Deception in Research Involving Mental Stress

The topic of deception in psychological research has been discussed in Section 3-4. Deserving special mention here, however, is an aspect of deception involved in studies where psychological stress is induced. Such studies, for example, sometimes attempt to manipulate anxiety level by forewarning the individual of impending electric shocks when, in fact, there is no intention of actually administering them. Rather, the research is terminated after the anxiety is aroused and the data on the dependent variable are collected, following which the person is told that the experiment is over and that no shocks will actually be administered, the warning having served its purpose by arousing anxiety. Here is an illustrative incident:

In a laboratory experiment, one of the manipulations involved causing subjects to believe that they were going to be shocked toward the end of the experimental hour. In fact, no shock was ever administered. After a rather graphic description of the pain which could be expected to accompany the shock, one subject—who gave the impression of being very upset—actually raised her hand and said that she wished to be excused since she had a weak heart and was fearful that the shock might be fatal to her. She was, of course, immediately excused, and as she left the room the experimenter made an effort to calm her.

In other studies the participants are given the impression that they are inflicting punishment on another person who, unknown to them, is actually an actor only pretending to be hurt; at the end of such research, the participants are made aware that the apparatus had been arranged so that they were really not hurting the other person at all. One such study is described in the following incident:

A major journal recently published a study in which the obedience of subjects to the investigator's instructions was assessed. The procedure included pressure by the experimenter on the subject to continue to "administer electric shocks" (not real) at levels well beyond pain tolerance to another person, actually a confederate of the experimenter. Because the investigator was concerned about possible psychological damage to his pain-administering subjects, he did provide "therapy sessions" for his subjects so that they could express their feelings about the experiment once they had been told its real nature.

Studies such as these, involving the deceptive induction of psychological stress, have been criticized as ethically unacceptable by a number of writers concerned with research ethics. Others defend such research on the grounds that it contributes to an improved understanding of fundamental psychological processes and important practical problems. When such studies can be justified, the investigator incurs a strong obligation to minimize possible psychological damage to the research participants.

Previous experience indicates that a simple postinvestigation explanation of the true nature of the study and its procedures may not be sufficient; it may be that some participants will experience greater stress upon learning of the deception by which they had been "taken in" than they had previously experienced during the main part of the investigation itself. It is the researcher's obligation to anticipate and ameliorate such reactions at the termination of the study.

G. *Problem of Revealing to the Participant His Actual Weaknesses*

In a number of psychological studies, the participant is likely to be made aware of unexpected personal weaknesses. In some studies, this awareness comes as an inevitable concomitant of participation. For example, the individuals in an obedience study may discover that they are capable of being quite brutal when so urged by an authority figure; or in a study on moral temptation, the individuals may observe how ready they are to cheat or to lie. In other studies the painful insight does not come from the participation per se but from the investigator's full disclosure at the end of the research to some of the participants that they did not do particularly well at some task.

Some commentators have argued that truth is intrinsically good and, therefore, new insights which research participants may receive into their own true characteristics are positive benefits much to be desired. Others argue that while this logic may be acceptable where positive or welcome insights are concerned, the uninvited and unanticipated presentation to research participants of negative, threatening, or damaging information about themselves is ethically undesirable. This argument runs that, while such insights may be appropriate to a psychotherapeutic relationship, they are not appropriate to the participant–investigator relationship. At the very least, the researcher must realize that such revelations are likely to cause mental stress to participants and that, therefore, it is the investigator's responsibility to anticipate this reaction and minimize it to the extent possible.

H. *Potentially Irreversible Aftereffects of Stress*

In some investigations involving mental stress the potential for negative aftereffects seems especially great. This, in turn, raises the question as to whether the effects may be irreversible. The following two incidents illustrate such a possibility:

A study was designed to test driver reaction to a sudden hazardous situation. The subject (driving) and the experimenter drove by a "construction site." At a time determined by the car's velocity, a realistic dummy was propelled in front of the car at a time that made it impossible for the driver to avoid hitting it. The subjects reacted appropriately, but, once told that the situation was faked, they frequently reacted bitterly toward the experimenter. Despite this, and other evidence of great distress, the experiment continued until the planned number of subjects (18–20) had been run. Later another small study was run. Ultimately about 30 subjects were exposed to this traumatic situation.

The work which seems to me to raise ethical questions of the most serious type occurred in a military setting. It involved taking untrained soldiers, disorienting them, placing them in an isolated situation, giving them false instructions and leading them, as individuals, to believe that they had caused artillery to fire on their own troops and that heavy casualties had occurred. The subjects ran, cried, and behaved in what they could only consider an unsoldierly way, and no amount of debriefing could remove the knowledge that they had done so.

Where enduring negative aftereffects appear to be a likely consequence of research participation, the investigation should not be conducted. Where such consequences seem possible but unlikely, cautious exploration with a few pilot subjects may be justified, but the investigator should be prepared to apply effective ameliorative measures should the aftereffects occur.

Section 8-9.   Responsibilities to Research Participants Following Completion of the Research

The investigator has the obligation to assure that research participants do not leave the research experiencing undesirable aftereffects attributable to their participation. Such negative consequences can arise if the participants are permitted to remain confused or misinformed about important aspects of the study or, more serious still, if steps are not taken to remove effects of psychological stress or other painful consequences resulting from research participation.

Sec. 8:   Clarifying the Nature of the Research to the Participant at the End of the Study

Committing human resources to psychological research is justified by the need to advance knowledge about human experience and behavior. The research psychologist has a primary obligation to conduct such research with procedures most likely to advance knowledge and increase understanding. As discussed above in Section 3-4, however, many investigators assert that the best research procedures sometimes necessitate giving participants certain misconceptions about themselves or about events occurring during the study. In other cases such misconceptions, though not deliberately induced by the investigator, occur during the course of the study.

The responsible investigator feels an obligation not only to remove any misconceptions which the participant develops during the research but also to provide a full appreciation of facets of the study not revealed during participation. These may include the full particulars about the problem under investigation, the broader significance of the research, how the research might contribute to the solution of the problem, and the value of the role played by the participant in this process.

In Section 3-4 above, we have considered in detail the various circumstances which may justify the investigator in sometimes inducing or permitting the occurrence of certain misconceptions during the course of an investigation. Whenever conditions such as these prevail, the investigator is faced with a number of difficult questions. For example, is he always obligated to correct misconceptions, even if he did not instill them deliberately? Is the investigator always obligated to check for misconceptions, even when none were deliberately induced? Must the lack of information or the misconceptions be corrected immediately or may the correction wait until all participants have completed the experiment—or until any given participant has completed all the sessions? Must the investigator correct misinformation or provide missing information even when this will be distressing to the participant? What modifications of usual procedures are required when the research participants are children? These and related questions identify the central concern of this section.

Incidents

1.   I used a projective test which is a measure of masculinity-femininity. Since I did not want it known that this was an M-F measure, I did not so describe it in administration or feedback to the participants. (Explanation to the participants, in terms of use of space, expressiveness, etc., seems always satisfactory to them, thus far.)

There are many paper-and-pencil tests where the purpose is disguised, M-F tests being a group of these. Because M-F is such a loaded concept in our culture, I am particularly careful not to let data from these measures be identified. It is my practice to use code numbers wherever possible.

2.   To study the efficacy of counterattitudinal role playing in resolving social conflicts, members of rival street gangs were induced to participate together in a session involving this technique. However, the purpose of the experiment and the possibility that the technique would reduce conflict between the hostile gangs was not revealed to the members on the grounds that, however much the individuals really may have wanted to reduce the conflict level, they would suffer too much loss of face if they participated knowingly in a procedure designed to reduce hostility with the enemy gang.

3.   An investigator was studying immediate recall by presenting series of letters to subjects, and after the series they were to write down how many of each letter they saw, for example, four A's, three F's, one L, and two N's. The task became quite difficult when the series was lengthy, when the presentation time was either very short or very long, and when rhyming letters (C, D, E, T) were used. The inability of the subjects to do well on the task was obviously upsetting to some of them. They would show signs of feeling guilty, depressed, or would withdraw; one could sense that their egos were a little bruised. No provision was made in the design and administration of the research for building the subjects back up again before they left the experimental room.

Principle

The need to conduct research in a way that makes it maximally informative and minimally misleading may cause the investigator to withhold from the participant certain information or even to misinform the participant during the time when data are being actively collected. Once this participation is completed, however, reasons for allowing the participant to be misinformed or uninformed generally no longer obtain, and the investigator is obliged to provide full clarification. This is especially important where continuation in the misinformed or uninformed state might have some deleterious effect on the participant. There are various reasons why immediate clarification is important. The longer that the uninformed or misinformed state persists, the greater the likelihood that it will be integrated into the participant's thought system, and lead to other errors or to inappropriate action. Also, the longer it persists, the more likely it is that the subsequent disclosure will have a detrimental impact on the participant's feeling of trust in interpersonal relationships. Practically, too, it becomes increasingly difficult to locate the participant and to motivate attendance at a session in which clarification may be presented.

Principle 8.   After the data are collected, ethical practice requires the investigator to provide the participant with a full clarification of the nature of the study and to remove any misconceptions that may have arisen. Where scientific or humane values justify delaying or withholding information, the investigator acquires a special responsibility to assure that there are no damaging consequences for the participant.

Discussion

The experience of many researchers attests to the fact that one is likely to encounter a number of difficulties and special problems in the effort to implement this principle.

A.   *Avoiding Angering or Disillusioning the Participants*

When planning an investigation which involves misleading or misinforming research participants, the investigator must be alert to the possibility that the postinvestigation clarification procedure may instigate feelings of anger and resentment in the research participants. They sometimes will feel embarrassed at having been deceived so easily. Sometimes participants feel resentful toward the investigator and toward psychological research in general. One such case is described in the following incident:

In a study done by an acquaintance of mine involving an experimental game, the subjects were told that they were playing against another person when, in fact, they were responding to a series of preprogrammed moves. Although there was an otherwise exemplary debriefing, the deception was not disclosed because the experimenter believed such disclosure would reveal the purpose of the experiment to other potential subjects who would no longer be naive. Also, it might anger those who had actually been deceived. This could add further to the general suspicion with which psychologists are viewed by the public. In my own research I have always revealed the deception, but after some thought have decided that my acquaintance was acting ethically and responsibly—that minor deceptions need not be revealed if they would not be discovered later and if the knowledge of these deceptions might increase the subject's or the public's aversion to psychology.

The possibility of such deleterious effects of postresearch clarification does impose on the investigator the additional obligation to consider alternative research designs. Moreover, it is essential to develop a clarification procedure that will not only leave the participant fully informed but will also minimize the likelihood of any serious resentment toward the investigator, the institution, or to the conduct of future research. In addition, the participant should not suffer appreciable loss of self-esteem or disillusionment regarding interpersonal trust.

B. *Providing Information Regarding the Outcome of a Study Once Data Are Analyzed and Interpreted*

Typically the researcher cannot provide information about the outcome of the study to the participant immediately after the data are collected. However, the participant's appreciation of his research experience may be much improved by providing him with the full report of the outcome of the research, or at least an abstract of it as soon as possible after the completion of the study. The investigator should consider the importance of such a report and, where it seems likely to be useful to any appreciable number of participants, he should collect information (e.g., future addresses) that will allow the report to be forwarded to the interested participants. In all cases where a promise is made to send such materials, the investigator must honor the obligation.

C. *Waiting until All Participants Have Provided Data before Any Are Given Clarification*

In some instances, the researcher may feel that it is advisable not to provide full clarification to any of the participants until data have been collected from all of the participants who will take part in the study, because there is the possibility that some of the participants might talk among themselves and convey information which would vitiate the study. Such a development is particularly likely where the participants are drawn from a small population (such as from students on a college campus), so that if clarification were provided to early participants immediately after they provide their data, they might inform the later participants, thus making their data wholly misleading. Here is an incident illustrating this problem:

Often a long time must elapse before subjects can be told the truth about the purposes of the experiment, because early disclosure would jeopardize the experimental procedures. Sometimes subjects are provided with a written explanation later on, but they seem to prefer an immediate, oral explanation. This, however, often leads to a quick and superficial account. I typically use such a skimpy debriefing in order to prevent the circulation around campus of rumors that my experiments are full of deceptions, and I offer a full explanation later on if the subject is especially interested. Very rarely a subject returns to hear the whole story.

Here again, the researcher's feeling of obligation not to mislead participants has no easy solution. He must either continue to withhold clarification from the early participants until all have provided data, risk misinforming the scientific community and the general public by utilizing distorted data from later participants, or develop some modification in research design which avoids the problem. The considerations that apply here are very similar to those discussed immediately below, in connection with withholding information until the end of the two experimental situations in which the individual participates.

D.   *The Multiple-Session Study*

In many psychological studies, it is necessary for the participant to serve in several sessions separated by an interval of time that may extend for a week or more. This poses a problem where deception, misunderstanding, or stress occur in the first session, and the investigator feels that providing a full explanation of what went on in the first session immediately after it is over will vitiate the usefulness of the data collected in the following session. For this reason, it is often desirable to redesign the study so that it can be carried out within a single session, with the participant not leaving the laboratory until full clarification is provided. The following incident illustrates this way of lessening the seriousness of the problem:

> In an experiment on the development of self-control, subjects were to be told that their responses were creative or not creative on grounds that were totally arbitrary and had nothing to do with creativity. This was to happen during the first of two experimental sessions. It seemed unethical to allow the subject to leave the first session after receiving the conceivably threatening information, yet the purposes of the experiment seemed to demand exactly that. I felt that a reasonable resolution to this conflict was reached. The two parts of the experiment were shortened so that the subject could complete the whole procedure at one session. In that way they could be debriefed immediately. The threatening procedure was retained, but possible serious consequences were prevented.

At other times, the demands of the reasearch may not permit full clarification until the final session is completed. In such cases the researcher must take into account the possibility that there will be deleterious effects from allowing the person to leave the laboratory in his misinformed or uninformed state, and consider the possibility of altering the research design, or even abandoning the study altogether. In cases where such conflicts arise, it is usually particularly useful for the investigator to consult with others, including those who are especially involved in the welfare of the participant, regarding the permissibility of providing the clarification only at the end of several sessions.

E.   *Incredulity Regarding the Postinvestigation Clarification*

Where the research procedures permit the development of unusually firm misconceptions in the minds of the participants, the investigator may encounter skepticism on the part of the participants when postinvestigation clarification is later attempted. This is illustrated in the following incident:

An investigation was recently conducted in which two types of deception were employed. The first was to read a false "report on his personality as evaluated by several tests" to the subject. The second was to lead the subject to believe that he was delivering shock to a second subject. Debriefing was extensive and included an explanation of the deceptive procedures and the reasons for using them. Two subjects still thought that the deception had been unethical. Another problem that arises is that of convincing the subject that the debriefing itself is honest. How, having been deceived once, could the subjects be sure, for example, that the "personality report" was, in fact, fictitious?

In cases such as these, the researcher must make a strong effort to assure the participant that the postinvestigation clarification is complete and accurate. Usually it is most effective to explain in some detail exactly why it was necessary for the participant to be left ignorant or misinformed during the process of data collection and to show that the circumstances which required the original deception are no longer operative. Furthermore, the investigator should provide the participant with ample opportunity to raise additional questions which then should be fully, honestly, and convincingly answered. Persisting doubts by participants during "debriefing" raise serious questions, moreover, about the ethical acceptability of the deceptions employed.

There have been reports of a few studies which involved the particularly reprehensible practice of "double deception." This practice involves a second deception presented as a part of what the participant thinks is the official postinvestigation clarification procedure. Then some further measurement is made, usually using covert means to assess the impact of the conditions upon the true dependent variable. In such cases there is a particular danger that the participant, when finally provided with a full and accurate clarification, will remain unconvinced and possibly resentful. Here confidence in the trustworthiness of psychologists has realistically been shaken.

F. *Lack of Interest on the Part of the Subject*

The investigator occasionally confronts the situation in which the participant is not especially interested in hearing the clarification which the investigator had intended to provide. This is most likely to occur where the person's consent to participate was induced by some extraneous consideration, such as financial payment, or where experiences in the study were of little interest. In such cases the participant might prefer, if given the choice, to leave rather than to stay and hear the investigator's explanation of the study. Recognizing the value of research in general and the importance of the particular problem which he is investigating, the researcher should try to develop a postinvestigation clarification procedure that will suitably interest the participant.

G. *Special Considerations with Children*

The implementation of Principle 8 in research with children poses special problems. Because of their limited ability to understand complex explanations, the usual requirement for complete and accurate postinvestigation clarification of all aspects of the research process, including the removal of any misconceptions, may need to be modified. With children, the primary objective of the postinvestigation clarification procedure is to assure that the child leaves the research situation with no undesirable aftereffects of his participation. This may mean, for example, that certain misconceptions should not be removed or even that some new misconceptions should be induced. If a child erroneously believes that he has done well on a research task, there may be more harm in trying to correct this misconception than in permitting it to remain. Similarly, ameliorative efforts are needed when a child feels that he has done poorly. In some circumstances, such efforts may even include attempts to convince him that his performance was better than it actually was or special experimental procedures to guarantee the child a final experience of success. The researcher will usually find that advice on such matters from experienced colleagues, and others who know children, will be especially helpful.

The following incident illustrates a possible approach to problems in this area:

The experiment was essentially a replication and involved the concept of vicarious reinforcement. Specifically, would children who perform a task after observing another child being punished while performing that task do better or worse than a group which has not witnessed punishment in conjunction with the task?

Children were run in pairs, and one condition involved telling the first member of the pair that he was not performing well. We employed a simple motor task that involved dropping marbles through holes. The children generally reached maximum performance in about three minutes, and were told that they were not doing well. Since the time for each pair was six minutes, a great number of kindergarten children who were trying their very best were scolded for three minutes. Their anxiety was quite pronounced.

We ran the subjects as described, and lavishly praised the children after the ordeal, explaining that we were fooling. Most seemed to understand and were relieved, but while the condition was being run I had my doubts about whether it was ethical to subject children to psychological torment.

Sec. 9:   Removal of Stress and Other Undesirable
Consequences of Research Participation

A great deal of psychological research causes no appreciable stress or other major costs to the human participants. The experienced investigator, however, soon becomes aware that occasionally even the most innocuous research can inadvertently give rise to stress and leave the participant feeling anxious or inadequate. Simple cognitive tasks involving short-term memory or decision making can leave the individual worried about possibly performing quite poorly; or filling out harmless personality inventories may induce in the participant worries about whether he has some unsuspected pathological symptoms. Similarly, painless physiological recording devices may result in the participant's feeling frightened and perhaps worried that he lacks courage. Children, owing to their more limited range of experience, are particularly likely to misunderstand research procedures or to misinterpret, in highly surprising ways, routines and procedures that seem quite unthreatening to the investigator.

The humane researcher designs the study so as to minimize the likelihood of such undesirable side effects. Even after taking appropriate precautions, it is necessary to remain sensitive to the vulnerability of people to draw disturbing inferences from the atypical situations in which they are placed during psychological research. This requires careful checking for possible detrimental effects after the study is over and being prepared to apply appropriate means to remove such effects when they are found.

In other research, stress of a psychological or physical nature occurs not by inadvertence, but as an intrinsic and deliberately planned part of the investigation. Included here are studies involving the effects of pain or failure which were discussed in Section 7 on protection from physical and mental stress. Assuming that such studies are done, the ethical investigator is careful to remove any detrimental effects they produce as soon as the study is completed.

Finally, there are a number of related problems, such as withholding beneficial treatment from control subjects and whether, when possibly damaging information about the participant emerges during the research, this ought to be withheld from the person.

Incidents

1. I was involved in a study of the effects of pornography that extended over a considerable period of time, and I was worried over the question of whether the procedure would have any detrimental long-term effect. As a result, we used several procedures to guard against possible legal and medical problems: (a) The subjects were fully informed of the nature of the experiment; they were given the actual research proposal to read and were allowed to delay making a decision until they had had a chance to think about it. (b) All subjects were over 21 and were free of psychological problems (determined by a psychiatric interview). (c) Day-by-day monitoring by Clyde Mood Scales was carried out throughout the study. (d) Subjects always were aware that psychiatric advice was available to them if they needed it. (e) All subjects were carefully screened at the end to make certain that no detrimental effects had occurred. (f) All subjects were interviewed eight weeks after the end of the project once again to make sure that no harmful effects had occurred.

2. Students in a school of education were told by the experimenter that questionnaires revealed that they were unsuited for the teaching profession, although this was untrue. The expectation was that students with such evaluations would do poorly in their course work, because these negative appraisals would lower their self-esteem. Many of the students were upset with the

"results" of the questionnaire and considered abandoning the teaching profession.

3.   A graduate student in another department, to whom I was a technical (instrumentation) consultant, had one subject (an eight-year-old child) who experienced a severe emotional trauma during the experiment. During the experimental session the subject "went to pieces," left the room and returned home without the experimenter's understanding what was wrong. The procedure involved GSR recording. Only later did the experimenter learn that the child believed that blood was being drawn from his hand. The electrode wires were red plastic insulated and the write-out was in red ink. Although this was an isolated case, I protested to the candidate's advisor that insufficient explanation was being given to the subjects. How he disposed of the matter I do not know.

4.   Phenothiazines have been shown to be more effective than placebos in treatment of acute schizophrenia. Yet, in most research involving this drug, it is necessary to employ a placebo group. The ethical question is that of withholding a treatment of known efficacy in order to answer questions of scientific interest. Practices differ from one setting to another. The issue is usually resolved on the basis of politics and power rather than ethics.

Principle

Sometimes intentionally and sometimes unintentionally, an investigator may use research procedures that produce negative aftereffects in the research participants. Given that this will happen, it is necessary that researchers become alert to such developments. Once they are detected, it is obligatory that efforts be made to remove them.

Principle 9.   Where research procedures may result in undesirable consequences for the participant, the investigator has the responsibility to detect and remove or correct these consequences, including, where relevant, long-term aftereffects.

Discussion

A.   *Necessity for Immediate Removal of Harmful Effects*

In the previous section on removal of misconceptions, the possibility was discussed that under certain conditions it might be possible to withhold, temporarily, correction of misinformation that a participant acquires during the research, for example, until he completes a second session or until some other participants have taken part in the study. But where appreciable stress or other negatives costs are experienced by the participant, it is difficult to justify even temporary delay in removing these at the end of the given session. Where there is any possibility that the participants might suffer serious stress between the experimental sessions, even short-term delay in removal of this unpleasant condition is not justified. The following incident illustrates the problem:

An experimental subject came to me in an agitated depression the day after she had been in an experiment that falsely "revealed" to her that she was not intelligent enough to be in college. The study in question had used false feedback on a quasi-intelligence test to produce high-anxiety stress. No debriefing followed the induction of the stress, and the subject was released without explanation. The experimenter argued that disclosure of his purposes would have nullified the effectiveness of his procedures.

Incidents such as this illustrate the necessity of taking effective steps to correct stressful misconceptions, and to reduce psychological stress from any cause, before permitting the research participant to leave the research situation. The assault on the participant's self-esteem in this instance is hard to justify even if remedial measures were to be taken promptly.

B. Long-Term Follow-Up

Under a variety of conditions the researcher has to consider the possibility that, even though the postinvestigation treatment of the participants may seem to deal adequately with the stress involved in the participation, there might be some particularly susceptible persons in whom the study has triggered a long-term detrimental effect. The following incidents illustrate the problem:

I was disturbed by a research project on psychotherapy in which the residents of a state hospital participated. After the study was done, the subjects were simply dropped. One person, at least, who seemed to be improving ended up in isolation and with threats of suicide.

I have a personal acquaintance (a college student) who was informed, on the basis of false GSR data, of "homosexual tendencies." In spite of debriefing, this subject was seriously disturbed by the whole affair, and two years later, came to me and asked advice on how to enter psychotherapy. The experiment involved was important and is commonly cited in the literature.

The researcher is obligated to consider such possibilities and either forego the research or redesign it in a way (as regards research experiences, participant selection, and postinvestigation checks) as to make the likelihood of such long-term detrimental effects negligible. Long-term follow-ups may also be necessary to assure that such effects are not occurring.

C. Special Obligations Concerning Children

When children serve as research participants, the investigator assumes a special responsibility to protect their welfare. This responsibility is particularly crucial with regard to removal of possible negative aftereffects of research participation. In some instances, as illustrated in the incident above in which a child thought his blood was being extracted, the problem arises through the child's misunderstanding of some aspect of the research procedure. The researcher should monitor the experience and reactions of his young research participants closely enough to prevent such misunderstandings and their resultant unhappy consequences.

In other cases, the nature of the research problem involves exposing children to some form of mental stress, for example, frustration, anxiety, lowered self-esteem. The following incidents illustrate this:

> A colleague is doing research on the effects of fear arousal on attachment behavior in young children. The children are shown a frightening toy, and their behavior in approaching parents or other adults is observed. The ethical issue concerns the possible lasting effects of fear arousal. The researcher handles the problem by comforting the child after the experiment, demonstrating how the toy works, and allowing the child to operate the toy himself. Considerable time is spent on this postexperimental procedure, and, to my knowledge, no child left the experiment while he was upset.

> The tests given to the children were difficult ones, and no one could finish them all. Some children did very poorly, and it was obvious to them. Hence, we added a series of postexperimental trials for all subjects on which everyone was successful, in order to leave them feeling more confident and preventing loss of self-esteem in those who did very poorly. Yet we worried that in so doing we might be misleading the subjects as to their ability.

The researchers in these incidents displayed commendable concern for the welfare of the children serving as research participants. Similar postinvestigation procedures are mandatory in any study in which children are placed in stressful or failure situations.

D. *Withholding Information Damaging to the Participant*

At times the investigator may discover things about the participant that could be damaging to his self-esteem if revealed to him. For example, the participant may have performed very poorly at a task that he regards as important. This raises the question of whether or not full postinvestigation clarification requires the researcher to disclose such uncomplimentary findings even where they might be only incidental to the main purpose of the research, and where the participant does not inquire about them or appear to be aware that information of this nature has been obtained about him.

In such cases, the investigator becomes involved in a basic conflict of values between his obligation to inform the participant fully on the one hand, and his desire to avoid harming him in any way, on the other. The choice between keeping secret from the participant important, but possibly damaging, information or giving to him disturbing news that he had not bargained for in agreeing to serve as a research participant is indeed not a happy one. The wise investigator will avoid placing himself in this unfortunate position by anticipating its development and making a suitable agreement with each research participant in advance. The main criterion in choosing among alternate actions in such situations should be the welfare of the participant.

E. *Withholding Benefits from Control Participants*

Some studies involve the use of a drug or of an educational or therapeutic experience hypothesized to have beneficial value for those exposed to it. Typically, the research design requires that this procedure be withheld from persons in a control group. This situation is exemplified by the following incidents:

> In a research study, vocational services were offered to some children in the institution where I work, but were denied a matched group of control subjects in the same institution. The administrators of the institution objected because these services would be provided for some children who did not need them and withheld from others who might profit from them. Thus the control versus experimental group design was abandoned because it violated the basic tenets of the profession of social work.

> In my master's level research in 1954, I employed a double-blind design in experimentally testing the behavioral impact of the then-new drug, Reserpine. The patients in the study were "back ward" chronic schizephrenic and psychotic patients in a large state hospital. I do not remember a specific, isolated question of ethics arising as such, and yet ethical issues were involved in that the design of the overall research (which included a second study following mine), supervised by the chief psychologist, took into account that some patients would not be receiving the drug believed to be potentially beneficial during the first part of the study. Apparently for ethical considerations, the second study involved placing all patients on the drug and studying the final result (intragroup differences in behavior).

There are strong arguments, of course, for the ethical acceptability and long-range value of this type of research. According to one such argument, the research participants in the control group have lost nothing through their participation in the study. These participants, this argument says, have been deprived of nothing of known value; in effect, they have lost no more than innumerable others like them who are not in the study at all. Moreover, the argument continues, even if there is a strong presumption that the procedure being withheld from the controls is beneficial, some group must be deprived long enough to provide the evidence needed to justify wider application.

In connection with Principle 7, we suggested the advisability of the investigator using as a control comparison for testing the benefits of a new treatment, not a no-treatment condition but an old treatment of known benefit. When this is not possible, Principle 9 suggests that the researcher incurs some special responsibility to his control group members because they were participants in his study. Hence, if the new procedures do prove efficacious, special efforts should be made at the conclusion of the study to see that the control participants are exposed to them.

What has been said above stresses the investigator's continuing post-research obligations to participants in the deprived control group. There may be corresponding long-term obligations to the participants in the benefitted treatment group. For example, patients receiving special therapeutic attention or children receiving nutritional supplements as part of a research procedure may as a result develop special expectations and dependencies. Termination of the special benefits at the end of the research might be damaging to the participants even though in the abstract it may appear that they are simply left in their initial state or even benefitted by the temporary enrichment involved in the research participation. In weighing whether he can ethically undertake the study, the investigator must anticipate the growth of many dependencies and expectations and assess his capacity to satisfy them after the research is terminated.

Section 10.   Anonymity of the Individual and the Confidentiality of Data

The ethical obligations related to maintaining anonymity and confidentiality derive from a widely accepted rule of human conduct. This rule is that every person has a right to privacy as regards most aspects of life which only that person can give permission to violate. Various threats to this right of privacy sometimes occur in research with human beings. On the one hand, the investigator may obtain private information about people without their knowledge. This raises ethical issues related to informed consent treated in Section 3-4 of this report. But, in addition, the investigator, having obtained information about research participants, with their informed consent, may pass it on to others later. In so doing, an expectation of confidentiality may have been violated. Problems of this type are the subject of discussion in this section.

The central issue has many facets. For one thing, it is clear that maintaining confidentiality is more important for certain types of information than others. Religious preferences, sexual practices, income, racial prejudices, and other personal attributes such as intelligence, honesty, and courage are more sensitive items than "name, rank, and serial number." However, there are undoubtedly great individual differences in the resistance different people would offer to the disclosure of different types of personal information. This consideration argues for a conservative stance, according to which the investigator should be very cautious about revealing any information about research participants.

Another aspect of the problem involves the recipient of the information that is divulged. It is no doubt one thing to reveal to a participant's physician evidence of possible drug usage by the person but quite another to provide the local police with the same information. Either disclosure entails serious ethical considerations, but the potential threat to the individual is almost certainly greater in the latter case than in the former. Requests for confidential information may come from many sources—the research participant's relatives and friends, officers of the law, employers, school administrators, the custodians of data banks, even the investigator's professional associates. The demands can be so varied that no simple list can be exhaustive. Again it seems clear that the investigator must take a position that will protect the research participant from many threats to confidentiality, some of them unexpected.

In some cases the problem may arise in ways that involve valued groups rather than the research participant as an individual. Many people, by choice, might regard it as a breach of confidence for an investigator to publish information they disclosed which would tend to degrade their sex, racial group, hometown, or social fraternity. Such considerations mean that the issue of confidentiality can even come up in connection with the publication of research results without specific identification of the participants.

Finally, some particularly difficult problems arise when the investigator, often by accident, obtains information that perhaps *should* be disclosed either for the research participant's own protection or the protection of others. It is not uncommon for an investigator to learn that the research participant uses hard drugs, has suicidal thoughts, desperately fears failure in college, habitually carries a gun, or is trying to lose weight on a diet that is known to be dangerous to his health. What are the ethical responsibilities of the investigator who discovers information such as this?

The following incidents show something of the great range of ethical problems involving confidentiality that may arise in research with human beings.

Incidents

1.   It was necessary to obtain parental permission to test the school children, and after the research several parents requested their child's scores on the intelligence tests. But we had promised the children that no one outside the research group would be told about their scores, and so we refused to discuss individual children's results with their parents, even in a general way.

2.   A psychologist who was a full-time employee of a company conducted an attitude survey in one of the company plants at the time of a union organizing drive. The announced purpose of the survey was to disclose any sources of dissatisfaction with employment in the plant. The usual guarantee of anonymity was given to the participants. In the course of the study the psychologist was able to identify certain individuals or groups with strong pro-union feelings. This information, if furnished to the plant manager, could have been of value in combating the organization drive. The essential ethical question is the responsibility of the psychologist to his employer versus his responsibility to the individual employees who participated in the survey under a guarantee of anonymity. The psychologist concluded that guarantee of anonymity covered not only nonidentification in terms of specific statements but also in terms of identifying individuals as pro-union.

3.   Members of the minority communities in this city feel that any research that involves intelligence testing is almost sure to show their mean lower than that of the majority ethnic group's. Therefore, the minority members are demanding a moratorium on intelligence testing (or at least on reporting of racial differences) for 10 years so as to give present ameliorative steps a chance to show an effect.

4.   A depth study was done of a small village whose inhabitants were well known to each other. Detailed case reports were published with some attempt to disguise the individuals and incidents, without substantially reducing their scientific meaningfulness; it seemed clear, however, that any villager who

read the book would identify the sources of most of what was in it and that much conflict and hard feelings would result.

5.   In a clinical study involving projective testing of college students, it became evident that certain subjects, especially one young man, exhibited pathology to the extent that the researchers were concerned. I do not know whether anyone tried to communicate with the young man to the extent of attempting to make a referral, but he later committed suicide—which raised the issue for the researchers of what their ethical responsibility is (or how far it goes) when pathology is picked up in the course of fairly routine studies.

Principle

These incidents demonstrate that issues of anonymity and confidentiality are not as clear-cut as they are sometimes thought to be. To the contrary, there are plausible claims from many directions for information the researcher may acquire about research participants. Sometimes the act of protecting their identity and holding facts about them in confidence seems to conflict with the rights, rather than simply the desire, of others to know. In extreme cases, maintaining confidentiality may prevent actions needed to protect the welfare— and even the lives—of the participants themselves.

Despite these complications it seems clear that the investigator's primary responsibility is to fulfill the expectation of anonymity and confidentiality with which the research participant enters the research relationship. Principle 10 reflects this position.

Principle 10.   Information obtained about the research participants during the course of an investigation is confidential. When the possibility exists that others may obtain access to such information, ethical research practice requires that this possibility, together with the plans for protecting confidentiality, be explained to the participants as a part of the procedure for obtaining informed consent.

Discussion

The introductory incidents used to illustrate the problem of confidentiality were selected because they present the problem in relatively pure form. More often than not, as the principle implies, confidentiality is only one of a cluster of ethical issues that appear together in a research situation. The following incident illustrates this point:

An instructor who wished to conduct a study of the sexual behavior of women living on campus went through the following procedures: He presented a general description of the proposed research to several male and female faculty colleagues, graduate students, and undergraduate students whom he knew. He formulated the questionnaire by pretesting questions on this group, revising the wording of questions to make them as inoffensive and unembarrassing as possible (avoiding psychological stress), and screening out those which the group thought were quite likely to be perceived as offensive. Potential subjects were to pick up the questionnaires anonymously (confidentiality of data) and fill them out the same way. The procedure did not allow for later matching of the subject's name with her data (confidentiality of data). The subjects were also informed on a cover sheet about the nature of the study and that they could refuse to participate at any time they chose (freedom from coercion). When the research proposal was presented to the department's ethics committee, it was approved. (Parenthetic reference to various ethical issues added.)

A. Maintaining the Participant's Anonymity

The above incident provides an excellent example of how a sensitive ethical problem might be handled. So far as confidentiality goes, it includes a procedure that will always solve the problem. The data were obtained in a way that insured *anonymity*. Under such circumstances even unintentional violations of Principle 10 are impossible. Violations of anonymity which raise ethical questions are illustrated in the following incidents:

> On a mailed questionnaire, respondents were told that they would be anonymous. The researcher, "For your convenience," included stamped self-addressed envelopes. Each envelope had a commemorative stamp placed at a preselected distance from the upper corner enabling the researcher to identify by name more than 100 respondents.

> I was doing a job-satisfaction survey for a local concern. The replies were to be anonymous. I was informed that the employer had secretly marked the questionnaire to locate "troublemakers." I burned the questionnaire and told the sponsor where to place his money.

In research where the investigator secretly marks the protocols in ways that allow the identification of individuals after promising anonymity, he has violated not only Principle 10 but also Principle 3 relating to informed consent. He has also incurred an obligation to reveal the concealment and deception later on (Principle 8), something that may be very difficult to do.

The legitimate needs of research to link different bodies of data concerning the same individuals can be met without violating anonymity. The investigator may employ private codes (e.g., based on initials or mother's maiden name, birth date, etc.) provided by the participant. Or the participant may be asked to trust the investigator's good faith in maintaining confidentiality without anonymity. The subterfuges exemplified above cannot be defended.

B. Disclosure to Individual Third Parties

Turning now to applications of Principle 10 to various situations involving threats to confidentiality, we find that they pose a considerable range of problems. Typically, the kind of disclosure about which the research participant will be most concerned is whether the information will be made known to particular associates such as parents or friends. Sometimes this objection to disclosure is based on a fear of the damage it might do to the participant's relationships to these close associates; at other times it seems to be based more upon the embarrassment to which it might lead. Principle 10 makes it quite clear that the investigator should not give the requested information to these individuals without the research participant's permission. As the first incident in the selection above indicates, maintaining such confidentiality can often be handled in a direct and straightforward way, and few problems may be expected to arise.

At other times, however, the situation may be complicated by the fact that an associate of the participant (e.g., a parent) may feel that he has a right to certain information obtained in the course of research, particularly if he was the one who gave the informed consent for participation in the first place. In such cases, it is clearly necessary for there to be an understanding between the investigator and the third party from the beginning as to what information will and will not be made available during or after the experiment. It is to be noted that Principle 10 does not forbid the communication of information to appropriate individuals or groups. There are many cases in fact where useful data will be obtained and in which the research participant might benefit greatly from their transmission to a teacher or therapist, for example. What Principle 10 requires is that such data be made available to others only with the free and informed permission of the participant. In the case of data of great importance, however, the investigator may be under a very urgent obligation to obtain such consent. This is discussed later in a section on "deliberate disclosure."

Although they do not always qualify as ethical problems arising in research, it may be worth mentioning that several incidents reveal that a problem of confidentiality sometimes arises in situations where personality tests are administered by students to their peers. The following incident is typical:

> In doing research on projective tests, particularly the Rorschach, subjects were selected at random from the student population at the university. The subjects were not told that their protocols would be discussed and evaluated by a group of psychologists and students which included some of their classmates. Although anonymity was assured, many times the names of the subjects were used, and the degree of their pathology discussed. There were no repercussions from this, but it seemed to many of us at the time that this was unethical.

In this case, the psychologist who submitted the incident pointed out that such situations raise ethical problems because a principle of confidentiality had plainly been violated. Specifically, there is the possibility that embarrassing personal information might be obtained by the students' peers. Moreover, it seems unlikely that the students would have been able to give fully informed consent to the release of this information. Most of them do not understand the scoring and interpretation of the Rorschach test and would not really know what they were agreeing to if they consented to have their protocols used in the manner described.

C. Disclosure to Organizations of Which the Subject is a Member

Often researchers are asked for information about individuals by employers, schools, clinics, etc. Sometimes these are the agencies that initiated the research and are supporting it. These organizations may feel that they have a right to the information just as parents sometimes feel they have a right to research data obtained on their children. As was discussed in the previous section, Principle 10 forbids such disclosure without the research participant's permission. If no such permission has been obtained, the experimenter should keep the data confidential. As in the case involving parents, when research is commissioned or supported by organizations that might later request the data, there should be an explicit agreement in advance as regards the confidentiality of data.

Maintaining confidentiality may be more difficult for the investigator who is associated with the agency making the request. For example, the psychologist in the incident above who collected information about employees' attitudes toward unions might have found it very difficult to resist if his immediate superior had requested these data. In such cases, data-collecting procedures that guarantee anonymity are desirable if the research can be done with such methods. If it cannot be, the investigator has a first obligation to take steps to protect the confidentiality of the data. Failing that, he has a second obligation to inform research participants of the fact that their data cannot be kept confidential.

It is possible, of course, to imagine situations where the experimenter would be required to collect and transmit sensitive data and the participant would be required to provide them, the penalty for not doing so for both parties being loss of employment. Such situations are clearly inimical to the ethical conduct of research.

D. *Disclosure to Professional Associates of the Investigator*

The research psychologist is sometimes asked by a colleague for information regarding individuals who are also participating in the colleague's research. Furthermore, in many laboratories such information is kept in files that are readily accessible to secretaries, students, the investigator's assistants, or others who occasionaly might have personal relationships to the individual subjects. The following incidents illustrate the problem and also suggest some of the solutions that have been worked out in at least some laboratories:

We had a well-organized (though completely voluntary) subject pool among introductory students. Any researcher who gave a standardized test to a subject noted this on the subject's card so other researchers who used the same subject could ask the first researcher for the score. This avoided duplicate administration of tests and also allowed researchers to obtain such test scores post factum, if the outcome of their research indicated a need for such additional information.

Our longitudinal study of student characteristics collected a great deal of information over the years about the individual students. This was kept in unlocked files in the office. Hence, they were accessible to secretaries and to many students, and indeed the offices were often unlocked at night so almost anyone could gain access to them. When we realized the danger, we numerically coded the folders, removed all names, and filed the key to the identities elsewhere. Yet the location of this coding key had to be known and accessible to many of the auxiliary personnel in the research.

As these incidents show, the purposes of research often require that data be kept for some time in ways that allow the identification of individuals. Where the research participants do not have to be recognizable by name, it would appear to be sound ethical practice to remove identifying data from the research protocol as soon as possible. Where the names of individuals must be available, the records may be coded and the key to the code stored where it is accessible to as few people as possible. Investigators have sometimes taken extreme measures to assure the inaccessibility of the code in the case of very sensitive data.

E. *Loss of Confidentiality on the Basis of a Court Order*

The confidentiality of research data is not safeguarded in the law, although proposals have been advanced that it should be. Under a wide range of conditions, a researcher can be legally required to supply information about individuals to the police and the courts, even when it is collected in the course of research in which confidentiality was promised to the respondent. The problem becomes particularly pronounced where the information concerns illegal behavior (e.g., use of drugs, violation of sex laws, participation in illegal demonstrations, etc.). Here are two additional incidents that illustrate the ethical problem:

We were doing a longitudinal study of student behavior and, hence, had to keep the student's identity signs associated with each piece of data, even where it involved legally touchy matters, like drug usage, participation in illegal demonstrations, etc. Knowing that we could be asked by the courts to supply this information, we used a code number for each individual and deposited the key in another country. This procedure was expensive and tedious (and probably leaves the researcher open to contempt proceedings), but we felt it necessary if we were to safeguard our subjects and retain their confidence.

Another colleague was interviewing people concerning illegal drug use. Later, some of these people were arrested for illegal use of drugs, and my colleague was almost called as a witness against them. In fact, had they not admitted their guilt to the authorities, my friend would have had to testify. Later he stated that since the law did not protect his relationship with his subjects, he would in the future clearly inform all subjects that their communication was not privileged. He also stated that he would like to tell them that if he should be called as a witness he would refuse to testify. However, he felt that this would be unethical because it would be an unenforceable promise to break the law.

We believe that the implications of Principle 10 in situations of this type are as follows: When investigators collect information which has any appreciable likelihood of being demanded by the courts, they should make the legal situation clear to the respondent in advance, including the vulnerability of the data, any possible harm its revelation in court might do to the individual, and the steps taken to safeguard the information against such revelation. In this connection some individuals have argued that investigators should be ready to promise research participants to maintain the confidentiality of their data by refusing to turn them over to a court even if this meant legal sanction. This may not be realistic advice. Beyond that, given the legal status of data, the promise mentioned above is a promise to break a law, an action that investigators would have to consider very seriously.

There is, of course, one main thing that the investigator can do to protect the research participant. If the sensitive data can be stored in a way that makes the identification of individuals impossible, the problem is solved. For this reason, the ethically careful investigator should reduce these data to such a form as soon as practicable.

F. *Deliberate Disclosure to Avoid Greater Harm to the Subject or Harm to Others*

There is a reverse side to the coin discussed in the section immediately preceding. In that section, the entire implication was that the research participant was somehow being protected by the maintenance of the confidentiality of his data. But the opposite state of affairs may exist.

The psychologist may discover information that serious harm threatens the research participant or others (e.g., due to suicidal or criminal tendencies on the part of the respondent). To what extent is he permitted to, or obliged to, make these tendencies known to the research participant's associates or to the legal authorities, even though he has promised to keep all information in strict confidence? The following incident describes the ethical issue in graphic terms:

> During the course of a pilot research program, a series of structured and open-ended interviews were held with a number of state hospital patients. Preliminary to the interview which was being recorded, all subjects were assured that only one other researcher would have access to the tape-recorded material, and that the taped material would not be heard by another member of the hospital staff. Either due to the guaranteed confidentiality, or perhaps due to other factors, the interviews turned out to be extremely revealing. Since these were mostly mentally ill offenders with serious felony charges that had been dismissed due to their alleged mental condition, much of what they were saying would clearly have jeopardized their imminent discharge from the hospital. One such interview provided instances of considerably more severe psychopathology than I had suspected up to this time. There was no further development at that time, but several months later, the patient "escaped" (walked off) from the hospital and was at large for approximately one-half year. We had no word of the patient until his arrest became national news, when it was learned that he had abducted, sexually molested, and murdered a 10-year-old girl.
>
> Although I am sure that my own guilt feelings in this case cannot clearly be separated from my objective responsibility, I believe the general instance of the case where someone reveals clinically pertinent information (e.g., suicidal ideation, homicidal impulses, etc.) after they have been guaranteed confidentiality, does present a serious issue. In this particular case, it just so happened that the patient did not come right out and state that he had uncontrollable urges to kill a young female child, nor did any of what he said bear the remotest suggestion of such behavior. But what if he had?

If he had, it appears that considerations related to the good of others require the disclosure of the information to appropriate authorities. Similar considerations argue for disclosure when the investigator discovers information that the individual is a danger to himself. This obligation derives from more general ethical principles than those that are strictly limited to scientific research. Principle 10 does place a special obligation upon the investigator, however. He must inform the individual that the information may have to be disclosed.

The research participant should be carefully counseled about the limits of confidentiality and, in this particular case, the justification for transmitting information to someone else. The investigator also should realize that he may very well have incurred a responsibility for long-term follow-up attention to the disturbed individual as is described in Section 8-9 of this report.

G. *Loss of Confidentiality through Research Publications*

Particularly when the mode of communicating the results involves presentation of case material on well-known individuals or people belonging to a narrow population (e.g., an identified hospital or ward therein, or a small identifiable village), it is possible that specific individuals might be recognized and sensitive information about them revealed, either to professionals familiar with the research setting or the other members of the research population who might read the report. The following incident presents the problem in a way that reveals the great difficulty that may attend the investigator's efforts to maintain confidentiality:

We occasionally obtain information from interviews with individuals whose reputations are quite widespread. While we maintain strict confidentiality, in the sense that the names and addresses of respondents are immediately removed and no person who sees the interview after the interviewer has finished (e.g., coders, research staff) can ever identify the respondent without considerable (and specifically forbidden) effort, it is occasionally possible to identify a respondent with a widespread reputation merely on the basis of his occupation and some of the demographic data. We were alerted to the dangers of this problem some time ago when a respondent was extremely hesitant about being interviewed because, many years previously, he had been one of a number of persons described at some length in an important scientific work that had become extraordinarily popular. Although all of the usual methods of covering over the identities of individuals had been used, he had no doubt about his identity in the study, and it had had an unfortunate effect on his personal experience. (While this earlier study was not a case study, it involved quite extensive descriptions of persons and situations that made identification quite easy, and, indeed, I knew a number of persons who knew the true identities of individuals described in this study.)

The preceding incident is an extreme case and one that clearly raises an ethical issue. There are many cases, of course, where the data revealed do not constitute a threat to anyone's well-being. In studies of human sensory functioning it is actually a custom to report data by the observer's initials, a practice that very often identifies the individual. Principle 10 permits this, given informed consent by the person thus identified.

The same reasoning applies to the more difficult cases. When the mode of publication involves detailed presentation of sensitive data on individuals who are likely to be known to some readers, so that identification of individuals and learning of sensitive information about them is possible, then the extent of this risk should be made known to such persons and their consent obtained to the mode of publication, both at the outset of the research and after the specific report has been seen by them. Attempts should be made to disguise the individuals and dissociate sensitive material from individuals to the extent that this can be done without jeopardizing the research.

H. *Loss of Confidentiality through Data Banks*

A data bank is any collection of coded information about individuals that is kept in a form so that the information is easily retrievable, often by automatic means. Such banks serve several purposes. Those maintained by credit bureaus and the college registrar's office are of one type. These data provide a record of the individual's history of paying bills in the one case and classroom performance in the other. They are used to make decisions with respect to the individual in connection with some related concern such as admission to graduate school or extending credit. Other banks of data are developed for research purposes. Only this latter type is of direct concern here.

Data banks develop as research needs require the collation of diverse information about individuals, permitting important analyses that would not otherwise be possible. Problems arise when confidential, private, or potentially damaging information about a person is included in the bank, or when the cumulative data on an individual invades his privacy although no single piece of information is particularly sensitive. Even where anonymity is protected by not supplying information on the individual's identity, the additional problem remains that, once it is in the bank, use can be made of the data to which the person did not, and in fact would not, consent. To cite a pertinent example:

Our state department of institutions designed a study apparently aimed at surveying rates of occurrence of a wide variety of events and variables. An attempt was made to have all mental health clinics and institutions in the state provide these data on each patient and to include the patient's social security number. Our clinic staff strongly objected to including the social security number as this would obviously make access to the patient's identification extremely simple. It was the opinion of our staff that the information being asked for should remain anonymous.

Ethical concerns arise in these cases because the investigator loses control of his data. If the data in the data bank identify the individual, they may be used to his disadvantage. The data bank may be managed in a way that does not safeguard confidentiality. The researcher may not wish to contribute data to a data bank because people who will have access to the data are not adequately trained or motivated to interpret them accurately. Or the researcher may be reluctant to contribute to the data bank without having obtained informed consent to do so. Principle 10 seems to make the investigator's obligation in the situation clear. Research participants must be informed of the proposed use of the data, and their consent for such use must be obtained. In addition, before contributing information concerning individuals to a data bank, investigators should assure themselves that safeguards exist which protect the confidentiality of the information and the anonymity of the individual. In short, the ethical obligation to maintain confidentiality includes a responsibility beyond the immediate relationship to the participant.

Possibly the most common problems in connection with data banks will arise in cases where the investigator receives the request for data sometime after the completion of a study. The individuals involved would be difficult or impossible to contact and obtaining informed consent would not be practicable.

In such cases the investigator should consider the ethical situation very carefully and obtain advice before he agrees to release the data, asking such questions as these: Are the data sensitive? Is there reason to suppose that people would object to their being known to others? Is there any possibility that the information could be used to the individual's disadvantage? If the data enter the data bank will confidentiality *then* be maintained? Unless appropriate answers to these questions are forthcoming, the data should not be released to the data bank.

I. *Confidentiality of Information about the Subject's Valued Groups*

Sometimes there is a problem of confidentiality that involves the individual participant's valued groups. There is a concept of betraying confidentiality "by category" when research reveals things that may be seen as degrading these groups. The following incident illustrates:

> To study effects on racial hostility of attending religious and other types of schools, an anti-Semitism scale was given to pupils in public and parochial schools, in mixed urban areas and in more affluent and homogeneous suburbs. The pupils or their parents were not told the purpose of this when their consent was sought, and the results were published to show that those with certain school backgrounds were more anti-Semitic than others. Many pupils from such schools might have resented such offensive labeling of them in a general way by category, and thus the procedure may raise questions of violation of free and informed consent and of respect for one's privacy and confidentiality by category as well as by specific individual designation.

This issue, as portrayed in this incident, presents the researcher with a severe value conflict. On the one side is an obligation to research participants who may not wish to see derogatory information (in whose validity they will probably not believe) published about their valued groups. On the other is an obligation to publish findings one believes relevant to scientific progress, an objective which in the investigator's view will contribute to the eventual understanding and amelioration of social and personal problems.

Clearly the resolution of such a value conflict must remain with the individual investigator. It can sometimes be dealt with before it arises. When the problem may be anticipated before the data are collected, the investigator will be wise to include information about potential uses of the data in the explanation provided to the potential research participant at the time of his recruitment to the study. The latter may then give informed and uncoerced consent to participate, knowing in advance that among the research outcomes there may be one or more he dislikes. The issue, in fact, is perhaps better conceived as one of informed consent, not of confidentiality.

To make this suggestion is not to diminish the magnitude of the dilemma under consideration. The investigator must be constantly alert to the fact that many potential topics of study are emotionally and politically explosive. Just as he is sensitive to his scientific responsibilities, he must also be sensitive to the social, political, and human implications of the interpretations that might be placed by others upon this research once the findings have been published.

IV. ETHICAL ISSUES IN THE SPONSORSHIP OF RESEARCH, IN THE MISUSE OF RESEARCH, IN RESTRICTING ACCESS TO RESEARCH FINDINGS, AND IN THE UTILIZATION OF RESEARCH RESULTS

The ethical principles advanced in this document for the guidance of psychological research have concentrated on the researcher's obligations to safeguard the dignity and well-being of the participants. This final section considers several additional areas of ethical concern that arise in connection with psychological research.

The discussion in this section, unlike that which preceded it, is presented as exploratory only. It deals with matters on which a very wide range of views exist among psychologists, often arising from basic disagreements in social and political ideology. Given these fundamental but relatively unexplored disagreements on the basic issues, recommended principles for the profession as a whole cannot yet be formulated. Moreover, this part of the document, unlike the earlier parts, cannot be organized around incidents of ethical concern submitted by APA members. The project mission was to develop guidelines for the treatment of human research participants, and the incidents supplied by the members had primarily that focus.

The areas of concern to be discussed fall into four categories. First, there are ethical questions raised by the nature of the agency that provides financial support for research. Second, there are concerns about the misuse of research for purposes detrimental to human welfare. Third, there are ethical questions about restricting access to research data. Fourth, there is the question of responsibility for promoting the utilization of research results.

Ethical Issues Arising in Connection with the Source of Financial Support

The responsibility of the psychological researcher to advance human knowledge through significant and competent research often necessitates obtaining financial support from some sponsoring institution. Concern has been expressed that acceptance of such support raises ethical issues by associating the researcher with the goal of the sponsoring agency. The problem becomes acute when the agency's goals or means are widely regarded as objectionable, and especially when the researcher personally rejects the agency's mission.

Not all observers will agree on whether a given agency's goals are admirable or reprehensible and not all will agree even that the researcher ought not to accept funds from agencies with whose goals his disagrees. For some observers, accepting funds from the U. S. Defense Department implies endorsement of its military mission, while, for others, there is no such implication. And for some, contributing to the success of the Defense Department's mission implies noble and patriotic motives, while for others this same activity is reprehensible. Acceptance of research funds from certain corporations, religious bodies or philanthropic foundations would draw a similar range of reactions. Furthermore, the implications of accepting support from a given source undergo marked changes over time. In wartime, for example, the goals of defense-related agencies may be seen in one light; in peacetime many persons will take a different view of the purposes of these organizations—though, of course, others will not.

Questions to which the nature of the sponsoring agency gives rise are as follows: Might the agency influence the selection of research problems? Contrary to the investigator's intentions, might the research results contribute to the success of the funding agency's mission? Might the agency influence the outcome of the research? Does the acceptance of funds imply the investigator's endorsement of the goals of the agency? These questions are discussed below.

Most basic researchers would argue that the missions of the funding agencies have little if any influence on the selection of research problems. The investigator seeks a relevant agency after selecting the research problem rather than the reverse. At most, the agency's mission might influence the arbitrary details of the research, for example, a researcher testing a learning hypothesis may select materials to be learned that are relevant to the agency. But some observers believe that the channeling of research funds through given agencies does have an effect, at least indirectly and in the long run, in shaping the selection of research problems toward greater relevance to their missions. And in the case of applied research there is appreciably greater likelihood that the agency will influence the selection of research topics; at the extreme is contract research at the agency's behest.

Given that the researcher has selected the topic without reference to the sponsoring agency's mission, there is still the possibility that the research outcomes will contribute to the mission or else the agency would not be supporting it. Where the researcher has strong moral misgivings about that mission, this possibility must be considered. Some would hold that one ought not accept the support in this situation, while others would argue that acceptance poses no serious problem. Still others would say that the researcher should do the work provided its possible good effects outweight the possible evils; and many students of the current funding scene would argue that the mission of the sponsoring agency is a poor indicator of the uses to which a given study (especially basic research) will be put.

As for the argument that the sponsoring agency might influence the outcome of the research, the great majority of psychological researchers would agree that such a consequence would be ethically as well as scientifically unacceptable. They would take this position even where—and, perhaps, especially where—the researcher agreed with the sponsoring agency's mission. In the experience of most investigators, explicit interference by the sponsoring agency in the outcome of the research is exceedingly rare. However, some would argue that the subtle indirect effects of the sponsoring agency on the outcome of research are more real than usually recognized.

Finally, there is the possibility that accepting funds of the sponsoring agency will make it appear that the researcher accepts and agrees with its mission and thus lends moral force and legitimacy to that mission. Where he does indeed support these aims, there is no conflict between the donor's purposes and the personal values of the psychologist. However, should this not be the case, the psychologist may wish to consider the wisdom of refusing the funds. If the decision is to accept the funds, the investigators may consider the advisability of specifically disavowing undesirable implications thought to be associated with acceptance.

While guidelines are not available for the difficult choice between abandoning significant research for lack of needed funds, on the one hand, and being seen correctly or incorrectly as endorsing sponsoring agencies' goals and programs, on the other, several considerations seem relevant.

The first, as has been noted elsewhere, is the potential importance of the research outcomes and the gain to human welfare to be anticipated from applications of the research findings. Another is the relationship of the research to specific aspects of the sponsoring agency's program. For example, an investigator might refuse to take funds from a military agency for research whose application might increase the effectiveness of destructive weapons, while accepting from the same agency funds for research whose findings promise to increase the extent to which the agency is equalitarian in its operation.

A final consideration regarding sponsorship arises from the fact that the researcher is typically affiliated with an organization or an institution. Research funds characteristically go from granting agencies to institutions rather than to individuals. For this reason the implications of accepting the funds are felt not only by the investigator, but by other members of his institution. Many of these members may strongly reject affiliation with the sponsoring agency. As a result, in making his decision, the research psychologist must weigh not only personal views about the donor's program but also those of fellow members (e.g., students, faculty, other scientists) of the group to which he belongs. Having done this, the ethical decision about accepting funds must be his own.

Ethical Issues Raised by the Possibility That the Research Might Promote Undesirable Forces in Society

Foreseeable misuses of research results. Another source of ethical concern raised by research is the ends to which it might be applied. For example, may a researcher who strongly opposes a government and regards its policies as harmful, conduct research that would help that government stay in power and advance its policies?

Looked at superficially, the answer seems so clear that one could doubt that the question could ever arise. Why would a researcher go to the trouble of doing a study that would serve a purpose he strongly opposes, and how, therefore, would the question of the propriety of doing so ever come up? The possibility becomes real because of several aspects of the research situation. For one thing, it is often unclear how much a given study will serve some purpose even after it is completed, much less before the outcome is known; and this lack of clarity tends to obtain particularly with basic research. Furthermore, a given piece of research can potentially serve many purposes, so the investigator can weigh the good purposes it might serve against the harmful ones. And besides these ambiguities there is the tendency in scientific researchers, as with many artists and craftsmen, for their procedures to become ends in themselves. Finally, and more prosaically, the researcher's livelihood or social status may become so dependent on his research productivity that he continues the work sponsored by the agency even while recognizing that it is being put to uses he regards as morally objectionable.

This problem is sufficiently salient in the minds of some psychologists, particularly those applying their research skills to the solution of specific practical questions, that a number of incidents bearing on the problem were received. One investigator described a study measuring behavioral effects of chemical substances and noted that among the uses intended for the substances was the lowering of the will to resist and fight during war and riots. He wondered whether the substances might not be used in military or police actions to which he would be opposed. On the other hand, he expected that these chemicals might be used instead of more lethal weapons and hence lessen an existing evil.

A second psychologist faced a dilemma in a very different area of life. His research question was to discover the difference in effectiveness among missionaries representing a major religious society, presumably to increase the society's effectiveness in making converts. However, he had doubts whether conversion to a Western religion was desirable for the target group with whom the missionaries were working.

The investigators in these two examples decided to undertake the research described because of interest in the basic theoretical issues under investigation, but many of their colleagues might question their decision. In other situations, psychologists may strongly support the ends to which the research is contributing and so experience no personal conflict; and yet they may encounter the disapproval of colleagues who strongly oppose those ends. In either case they should reexamine their position, and there are several considerations which might play a part in the decision to undertake the work.

The overriding concern should be the welfare of persons affected by application of the research. In those cases where such application is clearly to the disadvantage of most of the persons affected, the psychologist should not undertake the research. In particular, he should guard against doing for personal gain a type of research he would otherwise refuse to do because of the harmful purposes it would serve.

In some cases there are many possible applications of the research; in such cases the investigator may decide in favor of conducting the research if he judges the potential beneficial uses to outweigh the damaging uses in magnitude and probability of occurrence.

Unanticipated misuses of research results. Psychologists have learned that the data they collect and the relationships they discover are subject to uses and applications they had not foreseen and of which they do not approve. The problem presents itself in several forms. One involves the unanticipated use of the data describing individual research participants. Earlier, in the discussions of informed consent and confidentiality, it was noted that the psychologist often finds himself in possession of facts about individuals and groups which might be used to their disadvantage by employers, law enforcement officers, news reporters, writers, etc. The ethical principles stated in those discussions obligate the investigator to inform research participants of the risk of such misuse of data; they also require protection of the participant's anonymity (and that of groups to which he belongs) in every way possible.

Often, however, the problem is not with misuse of individual data but rather with misapplications based on the conclusions and interpretations of the study. To illustrate, one psychologist faced the question of what a heavy-handed national government would do with the researcher's discovery that its philosophy of self-reliant nationalism was not being stressed in the nation's public schools. The psychologist in question reported his study with great trepidation: Would he bring punitive actions against the school system that was his research host? Still other psychologists have been distressed about the use made of studies of test performance, in which obtained differences between racial groups are used to the detriment of the group or to advance social policies that the researcher considers morally reprehensible. Experience has shown that the investigator's careful interpretation of alternative sources of the racial differences found in such studies will be put aside by prejudiced readers in favor of derogatory, racist interpretations. Or, even without such misinterpretations, the results might be offensive to members of one of the racial groups being compared. In addition, they might be misused to bolster actions involving economic discrimination and social exclusion.

When prior experiences show such likelihood of the misuse of research results, is it appropriate for the investigator to elect not to pursue the research? Which should take precedence—concern for what is felt to be the possible misuses of the research findings or the responsibility to contribute to the growth of human knowledge?

Answers to this question will differ because the personal values and judgments of psychologists differ. For some, a given anticipated misuse of research results will seem entirely unacceptable and highly likely. For others, the same misuse will seem unfortunate but neither very likely nor very damaging. One relevant consideration is worth noting. Research findings vary in their likelihood of contributing to generalizable knowledge. Where the contribution to generalizable knowledge is more probable, anticipated misuse in a specific instance might weigh less heavily against conducting the study. One reason for this, of course, is that as the implications of the study expand beyond the bounds of the setting in which it is done, there are more potential benefits to outweigh the likely specific damage of malevolent misinterpretations of the findings.

Ethical Problems in Restricting Access to Research Data

Granting proprietary rights to the founding agency. One of the most fundamental purposes of research is to advance knowledge and practice, and this purpose is well served to the extent that the results are widely disseminated. Many observers would hold that it is ethically reprehensible to restrict the availability of research data. For example, it would be argued that a person whose social and economic role is that of researcher is not living up to his obligations as a scientist if he does significant research and then fails to report it so that it is generally available for use. It would be considered objectionable if the researcher failed to publish openly and quickly because of sloth, discomfort at what he found, or for the profit of his sponsor or himself.

Yet many public and private institutions assume proprietary rights over the results found in research they sponsor. If a researcher accepts such sponsorship should he make and abide by an agreement with the sponsor that the latter can veto publication of research findings? Some psychologists have no hesitation in answering Yes. Others would argue that entering into such an agreement is morally unacceptable because knowledge should be in the public domain (except perhaps where it violates individual privacy) or because of the researcher's obligation to contribute to the growth of the body of knowledge on which he is dependent in his own work. Others take a middle position that the sponsorship can be accepted with limited proprietary rights such as a temporary veto on publication or a requirement to disguise some aspects of the data in the interest of the sponsoring agency.

Restricted access to prevent misuse. There have been occasions on which the researcher feels that the data have been misused by someone doing unanticipated secondary analysis of his results. Characteristically such reanalyses are done on data which the researcher supplied to a data bank or pooled data files. Earlier sections dealt with questions of informed consent and confidentiality which this practice raises. The problem considered here is that the investigator who has deposited data in a central file or data bank may discover too late that, in combination with data from other investigators, his results make possible analyses of questions to whose answering he would not choose to contribute. Should he object or, in taking such a step, would he be attempting to exercise an unethical censorship of the search for knowledge?

One example will make this dilemma concrete. A psychologist contributed to a pool of survey research data the data from his study of determinants of opinion on key social and political issues. Among his variables were religious and ethnic affiliation. Later he discovered that another investigator was using his data along with other data from the pool to determine the positions on various issues of the major religious and ethnic groups. He was doing this for a candidate for political office who hoped to use the results to guide his political campaign. The psychologist in question happened to believe the election of this candidate would be a serious blow to the welfare of the people whom this candidate would govern. He was opposed to assisting in any way with the candidate's election. Should he do everything possible to withdraw his data or should he take the position that to conduct the proposed analysis (and any others in the future), however much he disliked it, is the right of the other investigator?

Responsibility for Promoting the Utilization of Research Results

Paralleling the research psychologist's concern that if he conduct research of certain types it may be misapplied, is his more general concern for the proper utilization of research in the advancement of human welfare. This is encountered both as a general question and, with special force, in cases where one sees his work being applied either inappropriately or to achieve goals to which he is opposed.

Several points seem relevant to a consideration of the psychologist's responsibility in relation to the utilization of his own research and of psychological science in general. First, from the point of view of society, the practical utilization of science is one of its essential features. It is this rather than knowledge for the sake of knowledge that justifies support of science in the public view. It does not follow from this, of course, that all scientists must be personally concerned with practical utilization; to the contrary, division of labor between scientists who discover and those who engineer the application of discoveries has long existed.

Second, the motivation of many scientists includes a heavy component of concern for human welfare. They ask seriously whether their science is primarily advancing or deterring human happiness. For these individuals—clearly growing in number—a personal concern for the amount and kind of utilization of their research seems inevitable.

Taking such considerations into account, it is easy to see that different mixes of them will lead psychologists to different positions with respect to personal participation in fostering the utilization of their work. We may imagine that only extreme conditions will provoke some investigators to a concern for research applications, for example, the desire to counter the inappropriate interpretation of his own work in support of a practice he considers to be very harmful. For other investigators, however, we will find that doing research of any sort without concern for its application to human welfare seems to render the research futile and meaningless.

67342

152
Am3e

Date Due

NYACK COLLEGE LIBRARY
NYACK, NEW YORK

BRO DART   PRINTED IN U.S.A.   23-264-002